TEACHING ACADEMIC VOCABULARY K–8

Also from the Authors

Fluency Instruction:
Research-Based Practices, Second Edition
Timothy Rasinski, Camille Blachowicz,
and Karen Lems, Editors

Integrating Instruction: Literacy and Science
Judy McKee and Donna Ogle

Integrating Literacy and Technology
Susan Watts Taffe and Carolyn B. Gwinn

Partnering for Fluency
Mary Kay Moskal and Camille Blachowicz

Reading Comprehension, Second Edition
Camille Blachowicz and Donna Ogle

Teaching Academic Vocabulary K–8

Effective Practices across the Curriculum

Camille Blachowicz
Peter Fisher
Donna Ogle
Susan Watts Taffe

THE GUILFORD PRESS
New York   London

© 2013 The Guilford Press
A Division of Guilford Publications, Inc.
72 Spring Street, New York, NY 10012
www.guilford.com

Printed in the United States of America

This book is printed on acid-free paper.

Last digit is print number: 9   8   7   6   5   4   3   2   1

Library of Congress Cataloging-in-Publication Data

Blachowicz, Camille L. Z.
    Teaching academic vocabulary K-8 : effective practices across the curriculum /
    Camille Blachowicz, Donna Ogle, Peter Fisher, Susan Watts Taffe.
        pages cm
    Includes bibliographical references and index.
    ISBN 978-1-4625-1029-0 (pbk.) — ISBN 978-1-4625-1030-6 (hardcover)
    1. Vocabulary—Study and teaching (Higher) I. Ogle, Donna. II. Fisher, Peter.
III. Watts-Taffe, Susan M.
    PE1449.T43 2013
    372.44—dc23
                                                                        2013002074

For "la famiglia," Jim, Jake, Olya, Jesse, and Matias,
and my NLU colleagues, for love, support, and patience
—CAMILLE

For my sister, Jennifer, the geography teacher
—PETER

For my husband, Bud, who as a historian
continues to stimulate my interest in making social studies
interesting and accessible to all students
—DONNA

For Dennis, David, and Jonathan,
for showing me each day what matters most
—SUSAN

About the Authors

Camille Blachowicz, PhD, is Professor Emerita at the National College of Education of National Louis University, where she directed the Reading Program and the Reading Center. She was named Outstanding Teacher Educator in Reading by the International Reading Association for her research on vocabulary instruction and the professional development of literacy professionals. Dr. Blachowicz is the author of several books and numerous chapters and articles on vocabulary and comprehension instruction, as well as coaching, fluency, and other aspects of literacy education.

Peter Fisher, PhD, is Professor at the National College of Education of National Louis University. He is active in several literacy professional organizations and was inducted into the Illinois Reading Council Hall of Fame. Dr. Fisher has published numerous articles and chapters concerning vocabulary instruction and is coauthor (with Camille Blachowicz) of *Teaching Vocabulary in All Classrooms*.

Donna Ogle, EdD, is Professor Emerita at the National College of Education of National Louis University, where she codirects the Reading Leadership Institute. She is also Senior Consultant to the Chicago Striving Readers research project. A past president of the Illinois Reading Council and the International Reading Association, she is President of the Reading Hall of Fame. The author of several books and many book chapters and articles, Dr. Ogle has focused her career on supporting instruction that enhances students' thinking and learning across the content areas.

Susan Watts Taffe, PhD, is Associate Professor of Literacy Education at the University of Cincinnati. She has been a special education teacher and reading diagnostician and is regularly engaged in school-based projects focused on vocabulary instruction. Dr. Watts Taffe is the author of several books and many journal articles and book chapters and has served on several national committees, including the International Reading Association's RTI Commission, as well as on the editorial boards of several journals.

Preface

This is an exciting time to be writing a book on academic vocabulary. Interest in integrated instruction and teaching core skills in the content areas has been stimulated by the Common Core State Standards and by investigations of curricular continuity for a strong workforce (Programme for International Student Assessment [PISA], 2012). We are an author team with extensive experience in our own classrooms, in working in teacher education, in clinical instruction for struggling learners, and in professional development for inservice teachers, schools, and districts. When you examine the references for this volume you will see that we have often written together on the topics of content learning, technology, integrated instruction, and teachers' questions about vocabulary instruction. Having the chance to put much of this thinking together in a volume about teaching academic vocabulary has been a wonderful exploratory journey for us all.

In Chapter 1, we explore the multifaceted construct of academic vocabulary, share research on the topic, and describe how we have chosen to define it. We also present the challenges teachers face in teaching academic vocabulary in the real world of the school.

Chapter 2 describes how academic vocabulary is embedded in academic language, and how that language may present difficulties to students. We examine the nature and purpose of the academic language that students experience in schools, and then enumerate ways in which teachers can promote students' understanding and use of academic language in their learning.

In Chapter 3, we provide an overview of vocabulary instruction and some of the seminal research relevant to instructional practice. We also outline a perspective on comprehensive instruction in vocabulary for the elementary and middle school. Together, these first three chapters will introduce you to the ideas and vocabulary that are used throughout the book.

Chapter 4 addresses academic vocabulary in the English language arts. Since much of language arts focuses on words, word structures, and strategies for independent word learning, this is a core area in which students will develop tools to help them acquire vocabulary in other content areas. At the same time, this chapter treats the English language arts as a discipline in and of itself, with its own vocabulary and concepts required for reading, writing, listening, and speaking.

Chapter 5 takes a close look at the major areas within social studies and history where vocabulary is a critical component of students' learning. This chapter includes suggestions as to how teachers can make decisions about which words to teach and ways they can help students use context, morphology, and visual tools in learning them. Two larger frameworks that help students internalize vocabulary as part of their careful reading and thinking about content are also described: Partner Reading and Content, Too (PRC2) and Robb Gaskins's Action Cycle.

In Chapter 6, we explore key understandings about math and science vocabulary, including the complexity of the concepts, the semantic relatedness of many of the concepts, the multiple meanings that many words have, and the frequency with which students may experience the words. We describe important components of effective instruction, including repetition and review, manipulation, and visualization, and then examine how to approach word problems in math and how to teach morphemes in both math and science.

Chapter 7 addresses the role of technology in learning academic vocabulary. The chapter begins with a look at ways to integrate technology into vocabulary instruction across the curriculum, and then shifts to consider the new vocabulary associated with technology and digital media. This chapter includes several resources to support teachers at all levels of technology integration.

To support all the learning of the previous chapters, Chapter 8 presents a compendium of resources for teaching academic vocabulary. This is a material-rich time for teachers, both in print and electronic media, and this chapter provides guidance for you in exploring these tools.

ACKNOWLEDGMENTS

The ideas and examples in this work have been developed with the collaboration of colleagues, students, teachers, and other educators across the country who all deserve our thanks.

Camille would like to acknowledge and thank our colleagues and students at National Louis University, especially Ann Bates and Char Cieply, the educational leaders of the Reading Leadership Institute; teachers and administrators of Evanston–Skokie D65, especially Ellen Fogelberg, Kate Ellison, Connie Obrochta, Kelly DeRose, Julia Starenko, Colleen Kelly, Vanessa Herrera, Marie

Chang-Pisano, and Jesse Blachowicz; Charlene Cobb of East Maine District 63; Jim Baumann of the University of Missouri at Columbia; and all of the members of the Multifaceted Vocabulary Instructional Program team.

Peter would like to thank all the students and teachers who have developed and encouraged his thinking about academic vocabulary and language, in particular Catherine Bernard Petersen, Elizabeth Gates, Katie Brown, and Wendy Mohrenweiser.

Donna notes that Project ALL (Advancing Literacy for Learning) team deserves special thanks for the work done over 4 years in developing PRC2 and in piloting both instructional activities and assessments for the domain-specific vocabulary important in each instructional unit. We think particularly of the work of Amy Correa, Elizabeth Cardenas-Lopez, Debbie Gurvitz, Kris Utley, Carol Schmitz, Chris Seidman, and Margaret McGregor. We also thank Dr. Robb Gaskins for sharing a written explanation of his important framework for studying social studies, the Action Cycle.

Susan wishes to thank the many teachers and principals who have welcomed her ideas and so generously shared their own, especially Bridget Howe, Amy Wagner, Sue Sawyer, Ginger Patterson, Kellie Long, Melissa Doll, Tianay Outlaw, and Brenda Miller. She also thanks her students at the University of Cincinnati, Angela Kinney, Hannah Chai, and Maggie Lehmann, and her colleague in Minnesota, Mike Graves, for sharing their ideas.

We all owe our gratitude to the nurturing, encouragement, and editing of the estimable Craig Thomas; to Laura Patchkofsky for her expert and diplomatic guidance throughout the production process; to Marie Sprayberry for fine-tuning the manuscript; to Paul Gordon for his creative cover design; and to the staff at The Guilford Press for being such a great team with which to work.

This book has been a labor of love for us—love for the teachers who work so creatively and professionally in their classrooms; for the administrators and other personnel who support them; for the teacher-educators and educational researchers who continually examine, augment, and share our fund of research-based practice; and, most important, for the students who are our future.

CAMILLE BLACHOWICZ
PETER FISHER
DONNA OGLE
SUSAN WATTS TAFFE

Authors' Note

The preparation of this book was generously supported in part by grants from The Searle Funds at The Chicago Community Trust to National Louis University and from the Institute of Education Sciences, U.S. Department of Education (Grant No. R305A090163) to the University of Missouri–Columbia, the University of Wyoming, and National Louis University. The ideas presented are those of the authors alone.

Contents

CHAPTER 1

The Importance of Academic Vocabulary

A great deal is known about early language development, and in particular about the importance of having older family members immerse young children in oral language and model the value of language. It is also true that throughout life it is much easier for children to expand their vocabularies when they encounter new terms in engaging oral contexts, with many repetitions and concrete referents. Yet, in order to become competent language users, children need to increase their vocabularies far beyond what they use in oral exchanges at home or with friends. In fact, the majority of the words they need are ones they will encounter through reading and learning new content. These are often words that they find in written materials or hear used in school, but may seldom have the opportunity to use orally themselves. This is where teachers have a real responsibility: in helping students build their awareness of and interest in unfamiliar terms, in developing strategies for helping students learn new words and phrases, and in providing settings for using these.

ATTENDING TO ACADEMIC VOCABULARY

In school, science, mathematics, social studies, literature, and humanities classes regularly afford students new opportunities and challenges with language as they learn. A significant challenge is that many of the terms they encounter are not ones that they have ever heard spoken, and the concepts are often new and complex. These terms are generally what are referred to as *academic vocabulary* or *content-area vocabulary*. Academic vocabulary is developed best when teachers attend to the important terms directly, providing guidance to students in identifying and learning these words and phrases. Most of us learn academic vocabulary through reading, writing, and exploring new topics. Students need regular opportunities to learn strategies for identifying and learning words they encounter in their academic work as they read and listen (*receptive vocabularies*); they

1

also need support in being able to use those words as they speak and write about the content (*expressive vocabularies*). An added challenge in content-area learning is that not only are there large numbers of new concept terms, but the ways in which ideas are expressed vary among academic disciplines. So both the vocabulary and the forms of discourse are central aspects of language development.

Recent work with teachers (Ogle, 2011) illustrates how unfamiliar words create hurdles for students as they try to navigate informational textbooks, magazine articles, and Internet resources. In one unit for third and fourth grades on simple machines, each book contains challenging text. For example, in the "Axes and Plows" section of one book (Glover, 1997), students need to comprehend the following:

> An axe is a sharp metal wedge that is fixed to a handle. The handle lets a farmer swing the axe head to hit a log with great force. The sharp wedge-shaped blade of the axe cuts into the wood and splits it apart. (p. 12)

You might want to pause for a moment and check off all the terms that might be new or used in new ways in just these three sentences. Which words are ones that students might encounter in several contexts? Which are most likely to be related specifically to a study of simple machines? Some terms, like *sharp, metal, head, handle, swing,* and *fixed,* are general academic terms that students may encounter in many contexts. Others, like *wedge, axe head, great force,* and *wedge-shaped blade,* are more specific terms that are used to explain simple machines and actions. Some of the seemingly easy words are part of more complex concepts, like *fixed to a handle* and *sharp wedge-shaped blade.* This short paragraph thus contains many challenging terms, phrases, and concepts students need to understand before they can comprehend the passage. This type of dense vocabulary that carries the meaning is common in informational texts used in our schools. These texts clearly pose challenges—both for students reading and trying to learn from the materials, and for teachers who want students to master the concepts and the words that are the labels for these concepts.

The demands placed on elementary students in reading and understanding informational texts and resource materials are compounded as students move up the grades. Several years ago, I (Donna) worked with a high school industrial arts department as part of an all-school literacy effort. I asked the teachers to examine the texts they were using with their students, most of whom took the shop and woodworking classes because they were not particularly interested in "college-bound" courses. However, when we looked at the chapters of these texts, they were filled with diagrams and technical terminology. Each short chapter in the textbook on woods and woodworking had over 30 new words students needed to learn and master in order to work with the tools. In fact, there were more unfamiliar terms per page of text in this book than in the more traditional academic textbooks. In addition, the terms were used with great specificity in the explanations and directions for specific tasks. For example, one short chapter on sanding woods included these terms and many more: *grit, finish, moldings, delamination, burnished, prep sanding, endgrain, grain rise, compressed air,* and *card scraper.* It made me realize the tremendous challenge it is for novice learners to understand new content; each discipline demands that students attend to and learn the specific meanings of key words and phrases, and to ways of using that information in speaking and writing. It is part of teachers' responsibilities to help students anticipate the need to attend to, identify, and develop understanding of important academic discourse.

How do good teachers do this? Our hope, as authors, is that you will continue to ask that question as you read through this book and identify the chapters that are most pertinent to your own context and needs to support the students you are teaching. We also encourage reading this book with colleagues in your school because the development of students who are avid vocabulary learners takes a schoolwide effort. Students need to develop interest in language, to become attentive to variations in ways to express ideas, to look for associations among terms, and to become aware of the foundations of English in other languages.

THE COMMON CORE STATE STANDARDS

The recently published Common Core State Standards (CCSS) constitute an important new component of teachers' planning for vocabulary instruction. These standards, which are now central to educational conversations, prioritize the reading and learning of content in social studies, sciences, and technical subjects, in addition to traditional literature. The CCSS anchor standards for vocabulary acquisition and use state that students should be able to do the following:

4. Determine or clarify the meaning of unknown and multiple-meaning words and phrases by using context clues, analyzing meaningful word parts, and consulting general and specialized reference materials, as appropriate.
5. Demonstrate understanding of figurative language, word relationships, and nuances in word meanings.
6. Acquire and use accurately a range of general academic and domain-specific words and phrases sufficient for reading, writing, speaking and listening at the college and career readiness level; demonstrate independence in gathering vocabulary knowledge when encountering an unknown term important to comprehension or expression. (National Governors Association [NGA] & Council of Chief State School Officers [CCSSO], 2010, p. 25)

DEFINING ACADEMIC VOCABULARY

Some of you may be confused about the use of terms associated with the study of vocabulary. We often hear teachers ask:

> "What's the difference between *content-area* vocabulary and *academic* vocabulary?"
>
> "So just what distinguishes *academic vocabulary* from general vocabulary?"
>
> "Why does the new CCSS framework use the terms *general academic vocabulary* and *domain-specific vocabulary*? What differentiates *general academic* from *domain-specific*?"

We believe that the distinctions among these various terms, and particularly between *general academic vocabulary* and *domain-specific vocabulary*, are useful to recognize in order to structure effective instruction. These distinctions have been used for many years by secondary educators, but the more general term *content-area vocabulary* has often been used by elementary teachers and reading educators. Although identifying the vocabulary demands in content areas is important, it is also helpful to make a finer differentiation within these, because the tasks in learning and using general academic terms and domain-specific terms are different.

General Academic Vocabulary

General academic terms are used across many contexts, and students are much more likely to encounter them as they read and listen. Because they are not used in everyday language, these terms deserve attention. When teachers focus on them, this pays off for students over the long term. In the short selection about axes given above, there are several of these terms, such as *sharp, metal, blade, force, handle,* and *split.* These are words that students will find in several school contexts—especially in science and mathematics, but also in literature.

Domain-Specific Vocabulary

In contrast to general academic terms, domain-specific terms are found in much more limited contexts. They are also more likely to be highlighted and repeated frequently in content-area texts and resource materials. There are several of these words in the paragraph on axes: *axe, axe head, wedge,* and *wedge-shaped blade.*

Vocabulary Tiers

In making the distinction between general academic terms and domain-specific ones, the work of Isabel Beck and her colleagues (Beck & McKeown, 2007; Beck, McKeown, & Kucan, 2013) is helpful. Beck and colleagues have differentiated vocabulary into three tiers, or groups. This framework is also used in Appendix A of the CCSS to explain the differences in general academic and domain-specific vocabulary.

Tier One Words

Tier One words are common, everyday words that most adults know and use regularly and that children develop in informal discourse. These words are useful but not conceptually hard to understand. English learners (ELs) often develop mastery of Tier One vocabulary, and their oral communication abilities cause many teachers to overlook the need to focus more attention on the difficult academic vocabulary.

Tier Two Words

With respect to academic vocabulary, Tier Two words include terms encountered in school learning that appear across several topics and content areas; these are words with real utility for students. Their meanings many vary by context; for example, the word *operation* has one meaning in mathematics, another in medicine, and yet another in work with machines. The root word *operate* also can take on varied meanings—for instance, to manipulate a game board's joystick, to drive a motor vehicle, or to move strategically in social situations. These terms are not used generally in conversational English; they are more abstract and are more likely to pose challenges to students. Therefore, there is real benefit in teaching Tier Two words, so that students can become familiar with the terms and develop strategies that help them unlock meanings in a variety of contexts.

Tier Three Words

Tier Three words, in distinction from Tier Two words, are more specialized terms confined to particular academic domains or content topics. They are often the labels for key concepts being taught in a content area. These terms are often introduced and highlighted in the printed materials and textbooks students read. Teachers generally also introduce these terms as they are needed for specific content development. As the example from the woodworking textbook illustrates, there are often many such terms, and it is the teacher's task to focus students' efforts on those that are most essential to the content being learned and that have the highest overall utility for the students.

Benefits of Using the Three-Tier Framework

Teachers can use these three tiers of words to think about which words to teach. Tier One words are usually (though not always) learned through conversations with others at home and school, and do not require much direct teaching. Tier Two words are those that we consider *general academic terms* and that require attention by teachers. However, because they often are well known by adults, many teachers think that students understand these terms better than is often the case. These words thus deserve teachers' careful attention.

Tier Three words can be associated with the terms *domain-specific vocabulary, content-specific vocabulary* (Hiebert & Lubliner, 2008), or *technical vocabulary* (Fisher & Frey, 2008). In this book, we use the term *domain-specific vocabulary*; this use fits the distinction in the CCSS documents between academic and domain-specific vocabulary. The domain-specific words have less general applicability, but are often central to the concepts and ideas in content-area instruction.

Other Dimensions of Academic Vocabulary

Attention to academic vocabulary has led some researchers to further differentiate some categories of words that are helpful for teacher consideration. Both Hiebert and Lubliner (2008) and Baumann and Graves (2010) extract a set of words that are most useful in school tasks and in thinking about state and national standards. Hiebert and Lubliner call these *school terms*, and Baumann and Graves use the word *metalanguage* to identify this set of terms, which includes words like *genre, estimate, summarize, draft, compare and contrast,* and *punctuate.* These terms are particularly important for students in the upper elementary grades to learn, as they are used regularly on standardized tests and other performance tasks. Many students have fairly "fuzzy" ideas of what they may be asked to do on such tasks and do less well than they are able to, simply because they don't fully understand the tasks' demands.

It is worthwhile to mention "up front" the difference between how general academic vocabulary works in literature and how it works in other disciplines. In literature, Tier Two and Tier Three words (general academic terms and domain-specific terms) don't occur as major concept terms, but are likely to be words that describe characters, settings, or aspects of conflict and style. Hiebert and Lubliner (2008) distinguish these terms because these are words authors of children's and young adult literature use in their work to "describe characters, their actions and settings in which the actions occur" (p. 111). These specific descriptive words (often adjectives and verbs) are often essential to understanding basic elements of a piece of literature, yet don't occur frequently within any one text. For example, the teachers' guide (Harcourt Brace, 1995, p. 640) for a third- to fourth-grade Encyclopedia Brown story by Donald Sobol ("The Case of the Million Pesos") suggests teaching these key words: *international, double, discouraged, fielded, testify,* and *framed*. These words help describe the setting and the problem, but are not repeated frequently in the story. The challenge such words pose to teachers of literary works is real: The words need to be taught, but they are often not related to each other and occur infrequently. In Chapter 4 of this book, we elaborate on how to address this challenge.

Identifying Important Academic Terms

Academic terms are identified and defined in various ways in textbooks and supplemental materials. Students need to learn how to use these different types of supports: italicized and boldfaced terms, footnotes or side notes, glossaries, lists of key terms with some activities to focus students' attention on the initial pages of each chapter, and so on. Some newer science programs include vocabulary cards with key academic terms and online games to help reinforce word learning. Reading and literature programs often focus on vocabulary to be learned, and some even teach students how to look at word families and make connections among terms. Teachers need to take advantage of these resources when they are available.

If you are not using a text-based or commercial approach to teaching, then some more general resources can be helpful in determining which words deserve focus. A useful, if somewhat dated, corpus of words was compiled by Marzano (2004) after the first round of state and content-area standards. Marzano analyzed the standards documents and compiled a list of academic terms that occur most frequently, organized by grade bands and content areas. This resource is still useful to check to see whether widely used academic terms are being taught in your classroom and school.

Another useful list is one compiled by Coxhead (2000). Her Academic Word List was derived from her analysis of 3.5 million words used in texts across content areas. (One caveat is that these were college-level texts; another is that the texts were from England and New Zealand.) Words found in the first 2,000 most commonly used terms in English were omitted, and then the terms that occurred at least 100 times were grouped into 570 word families (the stem, inflected forms, and forms with prefixes and suffixes). These words constitute about 10% of the words in content-area texts, so Coxhead's list remains a useful reference. The list has been used widely as a guide to academic vocabulary development and to determining the difficulty of materials. However, Scott, Flinspach, and Vevea (2011) found that only 12% of the academic terms identified as important in fourth- and fifth-grade science and math textbooks were on this list. Therefore, it is important to use the Marzano and Coxhead lists as starting points, but to be most attentive to the particular concepts and terminology used in your own context.

In this book, we too provide several valuable tools you can use to determine which words are worth teaching at particular levels and in specific contents. Because there are varied criteria for what is important across the content areas, these issues are addressed in the specific content chapters.

Why Academic Vocabulary Deserves Attention

You may be reading this book because you have become aware of just how much students' understanding of the content you are teaching depends on their command of the vocabulary in the materials you use and in the activities you develop. Research over many years has confirmed your perceptions: There is a strong correlation between students' vocabulary knowledge and their success as readers and learners. However, this topic may be fairly new to you. Our hope is that you will both read these chapters closely, and also reflect on the vocabulary knowledge and learning your students need to be successful in your classroom and school.

How Do Students Develop Rich Vocabularies?

One clear avenue for vocabulary development is wide reading. Nagy, Anderson, and Herman (1987) found that students who read the most were those whose vocabularies grew most over their elementary school years. However, Nagy (1988) also concluded from his research that students only learn about 1 of every 20 new words they encounter while reading. Cunningham (2005) explains this impact on students' learning:

> For example, the average fifth-grader reads approximately one million words of text a year and approximately 2 percent of these words are "unfamiliar" to the child. If 1 out of every 20 of those unfamiliar words is incorporated into the child's lexicon then the average fifth-grader learns approximately 1,000 words a year through reading. (p. 48)

Although this is impressive, it does not provide the depth of vocabulary learning students need to be successful learners in social studies, science, math, and all the specific areas they pursue in elementary grades. This is why Nagy (1988) concluded that the best vocabulary learning comes when students connect words with similar roots and base words, think of related terms, and use word knowledge (structure, affixes, and histories) to unlock unfamiliar terms. We agree that building students' awareness of how words function gives them keys to a vast array of words they would not otherwise be able to understand.

How Do Teachers Develop Students' Academic Vocabulary?

Although research studies confirm the importance of building students' academic vocabularies as a foundation for their learning content, most teachers don't seem to give much support to this critical area in their instruction. An observational study of fourth- and eighth-grade classrooms found that teachers spent almost no time teaching the academic vocabulary (1.4% of their time), although 12% of the time involved literacy activities focused on vocabulary (Lesaux, Kieffer, Faller, & Kelley, 2010; Scott, Jamieson-Noel, & Asselin, 2003; Scott & Nagy, 1997). Wright (2012) also found no direct attention to vocabulary in her recent study of hundreds of kindergarten classrooms. These studies may not reflect your own experiences, and it is very possible that the landscape for vocabulary instruction has improved. That is certainly our hope.

Given the small amount of time most teachers seem to devote to helping students develop their vocabularies, it is important to make that time most productive for students. Throughout this book, you will learn ways to maximize vocabulary teaching so that students can learn content more deeply. Both general academic and domain-specific terms require attention because they must be learned for the objectives of the content-area teaching to be realized.

The Academic Language in Which Academic Vocabulary Is Embedded

Students may sometimes have difficulties with academic vocabulary, but they may also struggle to make sense of some of the language in which that vocabulary is embedded. The languages of home and school are different, and it is part of our job as teachers to introduce students to the academic discourses of the various disciplines. They need to learn how scientists, mathematicians, historians, and so on write and speak about their subjects. Take, for example, this passage from a sixth-grade science text:

> Although water ecosystems, like biomes, have dominant plants, they are most often identified as freshwater ecosystems or saltwater ecosystems. (Watkins & Leto, 1994, p. 63)

It is unlikely that you would come across a sentence structure like this anywhere but in an academic discipline. If you were asked to identify the main idea, you might give it as follows: *Water ecosystems can be divided into freshwater and saltwater.* But notice how far apart the subject and object of this sentence are, and the information about *dominant plants* seems almost incidental. In Chapter 2, we look more closely at academic language structures and how best to address them. At this point, we simply want to draw your attention to the idea that students need to learn academic language in addition to academic vocabulary.

ELEMENTS OF A STRONG VOCABULARY PROGRAM

Basic Components

Some basic components of a strong vocabulary program are applicable across most content areas. A few of these are shared below, so that you can begin your engagement with this book knowing some of the foci that we elaborate more fully in later chapters.

First, it is important to analyze each vocabulary task both for the students and for the content you plan to teach. From the potential words, select those that have the highest utility within the lesson or unit, and those that have generalizability across other units and other contexts.

Second, you will need to help students assess their levels of familiarity with the terms and help them attend to those that are most important, so that they can devote their energy to learning those that have been identified as central to the content. You can do this in various ways including having students rate their knowledge of the terms; the goal is to draw students' attention to the most essential terms at the beginning of a lesson or unit of study, to help the students focus their cognitive resources where these will be most needed.

Third, you will need to use the opportunity at the initial stages of a unit to give students some instruction with the words. The nature of the activities will depend on what will benefit students most as they encounter the terms and discriminate their individual meanings. If there are many related terms, you might want to lead a lesson creating a semantic matrix highlighting specific attributes of each term. Or you might pair students and ask them to do a word search— locating the key terms in the textbook, and then sharing the uses of each orally. From this preview of the text, students could then construct working definitions of these words. This might also be a good time to do a lesson on morphology: Have students find words with the same root (e.g., *demo: democracy, democratic, undemocratic, demography*, etc.) and then decide on what the root (here, *demo*) means. Finally, students often benefit from a lesson on how to use context to build partial meanings of terms, and how to use the actual definitions texts provide.

Fourth, you will need to help students develop strategies for keeping these terms before them, for rehearsing them, and for deepening their understanding of their varied uses and meanings. Some academic terms also have more common meanings, and these different definitions need to be brought to conscious attention (e.g., see our *operation* example earlier in this chapter). These terms need to be used orally in useful contexts, so that students will develop access to both the written and oral forms of the terms. The interplay between using academic terms orally and encountering them in print is another important aspect of academic vocabulary development. Students need several opportunities to use new terms orally, to build a familiarity with the terms, and to experiment with the contexts in which they are best expressed.

Additional Dimensions

Activities that help students construct fuller understandings of terms than simply learning their basic dictionary definitions are needed for the students to really know these terms. Definitions or descriptions, attributes, examples, ways to distinguish a term from similar ones, and nuances of when and how the terms are used are all important. When students have opportunities to explore varied uses of terms, to both see and hear these words used in several contexts, and to explore online resources for the terms, students become more aware of how "slippery" definitions are and how important context is to word use.

Many academic terms have their origins in Greek and Latin, so helping students attend to morphology and word histories will build their understanding. It is useful to help students connect several terms with a common root. As Nagy (1988) explains, vocabulary development depends on students' knowledge about these morphological families and on their ability to use this knowledge.

In some content-area materials, visual diagrams of concepts provide important information about the academic terms and need to be studied. Students should learn to match new concept terms with their visual representations, and to create diagrams or drawings if texts don't provide them.

Supporting English Learners

ELs often are still developing their general, or Tier One, vocabularies while they are learning Tier Two and Tier Three vocabularies along with their English-dominant classmates. Because of this added learning challenge, it is helpful for teachers to provide sheltered English supports for them (Echeveria, Vogt, &

Short, 2012). ELs who have Greek or a Latinate language as their first language have a special resource that can help them learn academic vocabulary. Many English academic terms (Tier Two and Tier Three words) have Tier One analogues in these languages. For example, words like *absurdo* (*absurd* in English), *mesa*, *arroyo*, and *pacifico* (*pacific* in English) are common terms in Spanish, but not in English. Such analogues make learning domain-specific words easier for EL students when teachers invite them to connect both languages and use their first-language resources.

The importance of encouraging students to think in both languages is supported in a recent research study by Scott, Miller, and Flinspach (2012), who found that in their identified academic terms for fourth- and fifth-grade science and math, about 70% were Spanish–English cognates. With teacher encouragement, students can learn to draw on their first-language resources and find connections among vocabulary. Often what are more esoteric terms in English are more common forms in Spanish or French, as in the Spanish examples above. Simply asking students to make charts of the new words with the English and the home-language versions side by side can help both teachers and students find connections.

LAYING THE FOUNDATION FOR EFFECTIVE TEACHING

Teachers who are serious about helping students expand their academic vocabularies also create classroom and school contexts where attention to words is a regular part of school life. Being serious about language development also means enriching students' background knowledge about vocabulary, making it personal, and connecting it to their lives beyond school. Three aspects of engaging, overarching language culture are described in this section.

Teachers' Modeling of Continued Language Development

Students need your help and encouragement in attending to and learning academic vocabulary. Teachers are role models and guides in helping students learn how to be "vocabulary-smart." It is up to you to regularly note new and interesting words, as well as new uses of somewhat familiar terms, and to "think aloud" about these with students. For instance, bringing in a magazine article or a brochure and highlighting for students some unfamiliar terms as you read it orally to them can help students become more willing to do the same. As students move from primary to intermediate grades, some become hesitant to express their lack of familiarity with new words and concepts. Teachers can help students overcome this hesitation by bringing in words that are new to the teachers themselves, modeling how they noted the terms, and then showing students how they sought out the terms' meanings or engaging the class in trying to determine the meanings intended by the authors.

Teachers can also explain to students their own strategies for learning new words that are important. Some teachers may explain that they connect each new term to an already familiar word or experience, make a rhyme for the new word with something familiar, or connect the term to a person for whom it can be associated. For other teachers, holding onto a new word so it can be learned may involve creating a word card for the new term, putting the context in which it was encountered on the card, and then putting a description, definition, or illustration on the back side of the card. Some teachers like to keep a collection of words they are learning on their computers or smartphones. Showing students how terms are not just identified and defined, but then kept handy so they can be practiced, is a part of modeling how teachers as adults attend to new terms, develop understanding of their meaning, and then utilize strategies to retain them. Modeling how to practice and try out new words is important; many less confident students think that "smart" people learn new words immediately when they see them or hear them. If students are going to get into the fun of building vocabulary, they need to know that it takes many exposures and attempts to use new terms. Some students may be surprised that teachers also need and use strategies to learn words; it makes word learning a genuinely shared adventure.

Teachers can also encourage students to take risks in the classroom by bringing in and sharing words the students encounter in their own reading. This may involve taking time at the beginning of a class period to ask students to share any new terms they have recently found, and to explore the context in which the terms were used and what they may mean. Students can then use their own resource tools (hard-copy or online dictionaries and glossaries) to develop definitions for the terms. A class bulletin board or website of new and interesting words keeps the importance of vocabulary growth fresh and personal for students.

Still another way teachers can model for students their own attention to vocabulary is to read books about words and language orally (Braun, 2010; McKeown & Beck, 2004; Neugebauer & Currie-Rubin, 2009). At every grade level, there are both fun and informative books that can nurture students' interests in language. Some introduce interesting names and words, such as *Stereobook: Dinosaurs* (Schatz, 2009); some deal with the history of words and changing usages, such as *Americanisms* (Luke & Quinn, 2003); some expand students' knowledge of specificity of usage, such as *A Cache of Jewels* and *Kites Sail High* (Heller, 1987, 1988); and some foster students' urge to create new words, such as *Baloney (Henry P.)* (Scieszka, 2001) and *Miss Alaineus* (Frazier, 2000).

Nurturing Students' Interest in Words and Expanding Their Awareness of How Language Functions

Helping students become interested in words and language, and attentive to new words, phrases, and uses of language, is an essential foundation for vocabulary development. Students need to be interested in and knowledgeable about words and how they function as they encounter increasingly content-specific vocabulary. This involves teachers throughout the grades, from preschool onward. All teachers need to consciously check to be sure that they entice students with their own curiosity about words and help them explore unusual, new, and interesting uses of language. Although in later chapters we suggest many ways to do this, a good starting place is to check the collection of books in your classroom and tag those that deal with language and words. For instance, abecedarian or alphabet books abound in almost any content area. Examples include *The Butterfly Alphabet Book* (Cassie & Pallotta, 1995); *Q Is for Quark* (Schwartz, 2001); *S is for Scientists* (Verstraete, 2011); *Jazz A-B-Z* (Marsalis, 2005); and *D is for Dancing Dragon: A China Alphabet* (Crane, 2006). Brian Cleary's Words Are CATegorical series (e.g., *A Lime, a Mime, a Pool of Slime*; Cleary, 2006) is also very helpful.

Some teachers use magazines and contemporary culture to awaken older students to the creativity involved in creating new terms and revising uses of others. They involve students in thinking about vocabulary expansion by letting them find the most current words used for clothing, colors, hair styles, sports, and music. Teachers often have middle-grade students write a glossary of terms for their favorite fantasy series. In these ways, teachers alert students to the reality that vocabulary is not static, but constantly growing and changing.

The joy of exploring books, magazines, and newspapers with interesting words and with information about language should be possible in all classrooms, at all levels. With all the online and graphic resources now available, it is quite easy to build a collection that will entice your students and open new worlds to them.

Making Vocabulary Learning a Shared Classroom and School Activity

Several schools we know have weekly words that the whole school population learns together. These are usually words that have general utility across subject areas, but they help reinforce and develop students' curiosity about words and the wealth of words in our language. Some schools put these words on the school marquee where all can see them; others send the words home so parents can post them on their refrigerators. Many schools have students describe these words and use them in the morning public address system announcements. Teachers who post the words on their classroom walls help students maintain their attention to expanding their vocabularies. These are just a few ways in which vocabulary can become visible in a school.

In the following chapters, we share many ideas for making vocabulary exploration a lively part of classroom and school life. This is an essential starting place for all that we discuss as we focus on the central role of vocabulary learning. You may want to make a list of ideas that you have already implemented in your classroom and see how you can build on those, making them as effective as possible for all your students.

CONCLUDING THOUGHTS

In this first chapter, we have set the context and furnished some common vocabulary for what follows in the rest of the book. As you read on, think about how you can support your students in expanding their general academic vocabularies—helping them attend to, explore, and use an increasing range of academic language in their oral and written discourse. By identifying general academic terms as well as domain-specific words needed for learning particular content, you can then decide which words to select for more focused instruction because of their importance and general utility for your students. We hope that this introduction has also helped stimulate your own thoughts about the vocabulary-learning opportunities you can provide in your classroom and throughout the school.

DISCUSSION QUESTIONS

1. The CCSS include specific attention to vocabulary development. Examine the anchor standards shown on page 3, and think of ways you can both observe students' attention to vocabulary and assess their abilities to meet these expectations.

2. With a colleague or small group, examine a short section from an informational text (textbook or resource article). Then make a list with two columns: one for general academic terms, and the other for vocabulary terms that are specific to the content being described. Explain your choices to each other. Does the grade level or expertise of the learners influence these choices?

3. Reflect on the elements of vocabulary instruction discussed on pages 10–12. How do these parallel your own commitments and practices? What areas are different? What would you add or replace in this set of suggestions?

CHAPTER 2

The Role of Academic Language in Content-Area Learning

Amiddle school class was reading a science text about microscopic organisms. It read:

> Algae represent a primary food source for various aquatic organisms. Photosynthesis by algae also contributes tremendously to the earth's supply of oxygen. (Watkins & Leto, 1994, p. 236)

The teacher asked the class what this meant, and one student suggested, "The organisms release oxygen into the atmosphere." Although there are several complex concepts in this paragraph (*primary food source, aquatic organisms, photosynthesis, contributes*), the misunderstanding seems to have occurred not because of the vocabulary, but because of the language structures. Normally one would expect the subject of the second sentence (*photosynthesis by algae*) to refer back to something in the first sentence—that is, to act as a cohesive device. However, in this case the previous topic is not expanded; instead, a new topic is introduced. The confusion could have resulted from the student's searching in the first sentence for something that adds to the supply of oxygen, and deciding on the last noun, *organisms*. The language of science, such as this, is an example of the academic language that students will engage with as they work their way through school. It is a language that they are unlikely to hear in any other context. In this chapter we explore the nature of academic language, as well as ways to familiarize students with such language.

WHAT IS ACADEMIC LANGUAGE?

When students come to school, they already know a variety of language registers—the different ways that they speak to adults, to each other, to a baby, or to clerks when shopping. Once in school, they are expected to use and to understand school language, which is yet another register and a very different one. Cummins (2000) introduced terms to differentiate the types of language used in school and at home. He compared *cognitive academic language proficiency* (CALP), which is the ability to use and understand the academic language used for instruction, to *basic interpersonal communication skills* (BICS), which are the language skills a student might use in the playground or at home. In this categorization, in order to succeed in schools, our students need to learn CALP, which is cognitively demanding and academic, and which includes school-based discourse patterns. Often this academic language is characterized as *decontextualized*. Such language requires students to engage with ideas about people, objects, or events that are not present, and thus requires thinking beyond the immediate situation. Cummins's distinction was used primarily in relation to second-language learners, and is helpful as we think about the nature of academic language with all students. However, within the EL community there has been some debate about (1) whether academic language is truly decontextualized (Schleppegrell, 2004), and (2) which vocabulary and language patterns are academic and which are not (Aukerman, 2007). Coleman and Goldenberg (2010) suggest that the terms BICS and CALP have fallen out of favor because they imply a dichotomy that can be misleading. Although the general distinction is clear, the particular instances in which words and linguistic patterns are academic may be contextually defined by their use in the classroom. However, academic language is frequently regarded as the language used for instruction.

Other researchers and authors have attempted to come up with more detailed definitions of academic language. Some of them are displayed in Table 2.1. Though there are different emphases in these definitions, it is clear that they all refer to elements of language beyond the word level. So learning about academic language is more than learning academic vocabulary. It may also be more than being taught to be metacognitive. For example, Fang, Schleppegrell, and Cox (2006) argue:

> We have found that commonly taught cognitive and metacognitive strategies such as predicting, making connections, thinking aloud, inferencing, visualizing, summarizing, and dramatizing . . . are, although important, often inadequate to ensure text comprehension. We believe that children need additional strategies that can help them engage with texts with greater ease and critical mindedness. (p. 248)

In addition to being metacognitive about comprehension and vocabulary knowledge, students have to become familiar with the nature of academic language, including different grammars and discourse structures. Many of us have learned to do this unconsciously, but most of our students do not. So if our students are

TABLE 2.1. Definitions of Academic Language

Authors	Definitions
Bailey, Butler, LaFramenta, & Ong (2004)	The vocabulary, syntactic structures, and discourse features that are necessary for students to access and engage with their grade-level curriculum.
Chamot & O'Malley (1994)	The language that is used by teachers and students for the purpose of acquiring new knowledge and skills—imparting new information, describing abstract ideas, and developing students' conceptual understanding.
Scott, Nagy, & Flinspach (2008)	A register of English that has distinctive lexical, morphological, syntactic, and stylistic features.
Zwiers (2008)	The set of words, grammar, and organizational strategies used to describe complex ideas, higher-order thinking processes, and abstract concepts.

to become proficient learners in the content areas, it is not enough for them to learn the academic vocabulary. They must also become readers and users of academic language, which will entail some understanding of the typical functions, grammar, and discourse patterns in each content area. Such understanding has taken on greater importance now that most states have adopted the CCSS (NGA & CCSSO, 2010). The CCSS place a new emphasis on academic language in several ways: They place shared responsibility for the language arts standards with science, social studies, and technical studies; they stress complex text; and they focus on argumentation with text-based evidence. So in this chapter we explore the nature of academic language—its characteristics, its purposes, and its grammar—and we describe instruction to help students learn and use such language. (See Figure 2.1.)

WHAT ARE SOME FEATURES OF ACADEMIC LANGUAGE?

Some characteristic features of academic language are that it explains complex ideas; it often includes abstract concepts; and it represents higher-order thinking. It is important to distinguish here between the general characteristics (functions) of academic language such as these, and the specific functions related to some purposes for which it is used. We look later at the purposes for which authors use academic language, often termed *academic discourses*, and reflected in typical *rhetorical structures*, such as persuasion or exposition.

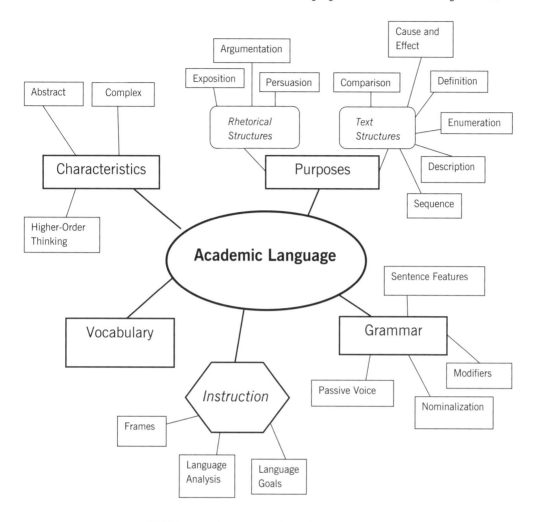

FIGURE 2.1. The nature of academic language.

Academic Language Explains Complex Ideas

There are many complex concepts in the different content areas (Schleppegrell, 2004), but there are also complex relationships. For example, students in science may be studying why and how lightning occurs. They need to understand the importance of, and the difference between, *positive ions* and *negative ions*. Other terms might include *crystals, thunderheads, kilowatt, electrons*, and *atmosphere*. Learning how all these terms are related, and how lightning happens, necessitates understanding the complex process of lightning formation. Similarly, there are complex relations in language arts between elements of a plot, the characters, the problems, and so on. For example, we often ask students to describe how an author develops the characters in a novel. Likewise, it is common in history to study the causes of events (e.g., the causes of the U.S. Civil War). In order to describe complexity, therefore, we need a form of language that is initially unfamiliar to students and that it is our job to teach them.

Academic Language Often Includes Abstract Ideas

Many concepts and processes in the content areas are not only complex, but abstract. That is, they may deal with ideas and objects that are not available to the senses (they cannot be seen, heard, touched, etc.). Although *positive ions* and *negative ions* presumably take a physical form, understanding the meaning of the terms, the relationship between them, and the impact on our world requires a high level of abstract thinking. Mathematics is another subject where abstraction is often paramount; teaching algebra would be impossible without abstract thinking. Students in most content areas are asked to learn abstract concepts, such as *democracy*, and to engage in abstract thinking about a variety of relations among some of these concepts.

Academic Language Represents Higher-Order Thinking

Several taxonomies of thinking have been developed over the years, but the most commonly referenced is Bloom's (1956) taxonomy, which was revised by Lorin Anderson and his associates to include remembering, understanding, applying, analyzing, evaluating, and creating (Anderson & Krathwohl, 2001). This taxonomy has formed the basis for many others, and is often extended and adapted (see, e.g., Passig, 2003). Whichever way these higher-order thinking skills are described, Zwiers (2008) points out that there is often a disconnection between students' thinking in their social interactions (however complex these interactions may be) and their thinking in an academic context. Academic language functions to develop thinking, although there may be different emphases on particular forms of thinking in the different content areas.

LANGUAGE, CONTEXT, AND THE IDEA OF LINGUISTIC REGISTERS

The idea of *linguistic registers* can help us understand how the lexical and grammatical features of academic language can change, depending on the purposes for which it is used. *Lexical features* are those related to words; *grammatical features* relate to sentence and other language structures. We all use different registers—for example, when talking to children, to friends, or to someone in authority. So a *register* is the constellation of lexical and grammatical features that we use in a particular type of situational context (Halliday & Hasan, 1989). For example, when meeting a child we might say, "Aren't you cute?", but when meeting an adult we are more likely to say, "How are you?" Similarly, when describing a seminar, a professor might tell a colleague when asked about it, "It provided me with challenging ideas about schema theory for my research," but might tell a nonacademic friend, "It was good. I learned a lot." The rest of this book explores some of the lexical features of academic language—that is, the vocabulary used for different purposes in different content areas. What we are suggesting is that students can become more competent users of academic language if they are familiar with the registers typically used in a discipline. For example, when students study history in school, they tend to think of the information presented in school textbooks as "facts" or "the truth." As teachers, we can perpetuate this way of thinking by testing knowledge of these "facts." But what we would like is for students to understand how historians select and interpret information in ways that are subjective and constructive. Learning about how historians use language for different purposes, and how it changes in relation to those purposes, can help develop this critical ability. In order to help them do so, we need to understand more about how registers work. As teachers, we need to talk about how knowledge is constructed through language in our different subject areas. It is necessary to make the link between the "content" and the language through which it is construed (Achugar, Schleppegrell, & Oteiza, 2007).

WHAT ARE THE PURPOSES OF ACADEMIC LANGUAGE?

Academic discourses may differ in their purposes, and therefore their organizational features. We can categorize these features in two ways: *rhetorical mode* (e.g., exposition or persuasion) and *supporting text features* (e.g., description or classification). Butler, Bailey, Stevens, and Huang (2004) found that texts in science and texts in social studies differ in their predominant rhetorical modes:

> The difference in the writer's purpose from one subject area to another is clearly evident.... The science selections analyzed differ from the social studies selections in that they follow a more traditional expository form in which information is presented, explained, and then sometimes summarized in a fairly straightforward format. The social studies selections, on the other hand, use a narrative form to present information. That is, historical information often reads like a story, unfolding chronologically with details provided through the eyes of historical figures. (p. 85)

Butler and colleagues (2004) employed the term *narrative exposition* to characterize this mode in social studies. However, they found that science and social studies texts *all* use examples of the same supporting text features: *comparison, definition, description, enumeration, exemplification, explanation, labeling, paraphrase,* and *sequencing.* Since these features are common to more than one subject area, teachers from various areas of the curriculum could provide instruction in their use. We have always taught students that all reading and writing should be purposeful. We have emphasized reading to understand an author's purpose. What we may have not done so well is to teach students how the discourse patterns that are the results of these purposes may typically differ between the subject areas.

Content-area reading texts frequently encourage us to think about text structure. They typically argue that we should teach five structures: *description, sequence, comparison–contrast, cause–effect,* and *problem–solution.* The recommendations are often accompanied by graphics, such as those shown in Figure 2.2.

In the United Kingdom, as part of the national literacy strategy, the use of *writing frames* is recommended for the exploration of various text structures. (We explore the use of frames in a later section.) We need to recognize that there is a difference between these macro-level structures and specific instances of comparison, definition, description, and so on, which may occur at the sentence or paragraph level. One of the anchor standards in the CCSS (for craft and structure) requires students to do the following:

> Analyze the structure of texts, including how specific sentences, paragraphs, and larger portions of text relate to each other and the whole. (NGO & CCSSO, 2010, p. 35)

Teachers in science, social studies, and other content areas now bear the responsibility, along with language arts teachers, of developing students' ability to do such analyses.

HOW THE GRAMMARS OF ACADEMIC LANGUAGE CAN PRESENT DIFFICULTIES

Researchers at the Center for the Study of Evaluation at the University of California, Los Angeles, have done several studies on the nature of academic language. They have looked at texts, classroom discourse, and tests to analyze the nature of the language that students experience in schools, and the ways in which this language affects their learning. For example, the purpose of one study (Butler et al., 2004) was "to describe the language of textbook selections in terms of vocabulary, grammar, and organization of discourse for test development. Specifically, the work . . . focused on the academic English used in fifth-grade mathematics,

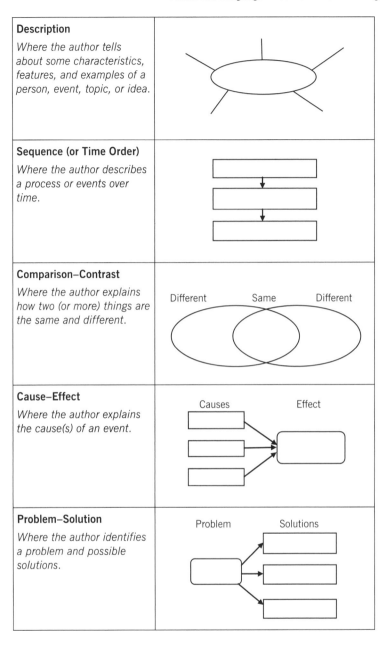

Description *Where the author tells about some characteristics, features, and examples of a person, event, topic, or idea.*	
Sequence (or Time Order) *Where the author describes a process or events over time.*	
Comparison–Contrast *Where the author explains how two (or more) things are the same and different.*	
Cause–Effect *Where the author explains the cause(s) of an event.*	
Problem–Solution *Where the author identifies a problem and possible solutions.*	

FIGURE 2.2. Five macrostructures in expository text.

science, and social studies textbooks" (p. 1). Another study (Bailey, Butler, LaFramenta, & Ong, 2004) looked at the oral language used by teachers and students in fourth- and fifth-grade science classrooms, and at some of the textbooks used in those classrooms. In these studies, Bailey, Butler, and their colleagues have looked at some specific grammatical features: sentence type, clause type, passive verb forms, prepositional phrases, noun phrases, and participial modifiers. Since many of these features did not appear commonly in their analysis, for our exposition we are collapsing them into four categories: the use of complex sentence features, the use of the passive voice, the use of nominalization, and the use of modifiers and modals. Before making general characterizations, though, we should make it clear that students will encounter increasingly complex texts as they progress through the grades. By the time they reach secondary schools, these features will be common in the materials used for instruction.

The Use of Complex Sentence Features

Academic texts, particularly at higher grade levels, tend to have long, complex sentences. Consider this example:

> Fearful of struggles like this one, European leaders formed close associations, called alliances, with other countries, agreeing to supply military support to one another if necessary. (Bednarz et al., 2003, p. 387)

In addition to causal links, definitional information, and some (probably) unfamiliar vocabulary, this sentence has an independent clause and two dependent clauses. That is, the complexity of the sentence could make accessing the content more difficult. Sentences like this, with subordinate clauses, represent hierarchical relationships that can lead to cognitive overload for those not comfortable with the content *or* the sentence structure.

Butler and colleagues (2004), in their analyses of fifth-grade texts, classified sentences into four categories: *simple, compound, complex*, and *compound/complex*. For our purposes, it is enough to know that a simple sentence contains one independent clause (e.g., *The temperature varies according to the seasons*); a compound sentence contains two or more independent clauses joined by a conjunction or punctuation (e.g., *The positive charges form at the top of the cloud, and the negative charges form at the bottom of the cloud*); and a complex sentence contains one or more dependent clauses, in addition to an independent clause (e.g., *If your hair stands on end or your skin starts to tingle, lightning may be about to strike*). Butler and colleagues found that fifth-grade materials in mathematics, science, and social studies contained mainly simple sentences, but a considerable number of compound and complex sentences. The mathematics materials they analyzed were word problems, so it may not be surprising that mathematics word problems were shorter and used shorter sentences than paragraphs and sentences in either the science or social studies text selections. What may surprise us is that there were not more complex sentences. The literature (Schleppegrell, 2004; Zwiers, 2008) tells us that complex sentences are common in the content areas. The explanation is, of course, the grade level of the texts: The higher the grade level of the text, the greater the number of complex sentences (Schleppegrell, 2004). Although this information about the grammatical complexity of text is helpful and provides a warning of possible comprehension difficulties, we should also recognize that grammatically simple sentences are not necessarily simple in their content (e.g., *Mimicry is a type of protective coloration.*).

The Use of the Passive Voice

Many of us first experienced extensive use of the passive voice when studying science. The passive voice in academic texts is used to represent a supposedly objective point of view, based on facts rather than opinions. We were encouraged to use the passive voice in our lab reports, to practice the discourse conventions that occur in "scientific language." In the passive voice, the true subject is relegated to the end of the sentence and is thus acted on, rather than acting. It takes the form (noun, object)(verb)(noun, subject). Consider this example: *Parts of an organism were replaced by minerals.* In this sentence, the true subject (*minerals*) is acted on, rather than acted. This issue of agency is what makes the passive voice difficult for some students to understand. Some learners, particularly those ELs whose primary language does not have a passive voice, may confuse the actor with the object of the action. Since passive voice verb forms appear in every four to five sentences in science and social studies texts (Butler et al., 2004), it would be appropriate for teachers in all content-area classes to introduce the notion of passive voice, and to explain how it operates to clarify or confuse content in their fields.

One way to help students understand the passive voice is to compare it with the active voice in sentences that describe the same thing—for example, *James put his bag in the locker* and *The bag was put in the locker by James.* The students can act out the event, which makes it clear who is the actor and what is acted on. Similar cameos can be used to reinforce understanding of, and to help students practice the use of, the passive voice.

The Use of Nominalization

Nominalization is the process of expressing meanings that are more typically represented in verb, adverb, or adjective forms as nouns or noun phrases. In academic texts, nominalization often enables something that has been presented in a series of clauses to be distilled into one nominal element. Consider this example:

> New tools, instruments, and theories about living things not only changed the way we classify them, but also gave us more organisms to classify. These *classifications* enable scientists to describe commonalities and differences between organisms.

Nominalization also allows a term to be modified and expanded. In our example, the term *classifications* could be modified to become *numerous classifications*. Another use of nominalization is to develop a chain of reasoning, as in this example:

> The ideas that are argued in this narrative are hard to believe. The *arguments* are loose and unappealing. The *looseness* makes the author's ideas difficult to follow. Their *lack of appeal* makes the document uninteresting.

Here, the verb in the first sentence is nominalized in the second one, and the two adjectives in the second sentence become nouns and the subjects of the next two sentences. So the process of nominalization across the paragraph lends coherence and structure to the argument. We know that students may struggle with pronominal referents (Bierwisch, 1983), and this additional complexity in terms of the cohesiveness of a text can be daunting. It may be important to help students to recognize how all these referents help to make a paragraph more comprehensible, and to point out instances in which they occur. But nominalization also condenses ideas, so that more may be expressed in a shorter space, which can lead to an even greater cognitive processing load.

When students read academic texts that use nominalization extensively, they have to understand more ideas per clause. They need opportunities to practice unpacking and translating these ideas, as well as recognizing why authors structure texts in a way that highlights new information and backgrounds what has already been said. In addition, nominalization is often used with abstract concepts, so that readers may be challenged to remember many such relationships as they work their way through these texts.

Fang and Schleppegrell (2010) point out that while nominalization appears in all content areas, it can serve different functions in different areas. In science, nominalization can commonly help accrue meanings of a technical term, so that it can be used as a summary of an explanation sequence, as in the example of *classification* above. In history, nominalization may be used commonly "to realize events as things so that historians can develop a chain of reasoning that at the same time embeds interpretation and judgment" (Fang & Schleppegrell, 2010, p. 590) For example, compare these two passages:

> If you look at bread mold through a microscope you can see tiny spheres sitting on top of thin stems. The sphere-shaped structures produce spores and are called *sporangia*. The "stems" are the bodies of the fungi and are termed *hyphae*.

> Toward the end of the 20th century senior workers, who had held jobs for a long time, thought they should have greater privileges than more recent hires. Seniority was often used as a criterion for job retention in times of restructuring and layoffs. The expectation of job security led to a lack of innovation as employers and entrepreneurs struggled with an aging workforce.

An awareness of how nominalization can make texts in particular content areas more complex or more comprehensible will enable effective instruction to make such relationships more transparent to students.

The Use of Modifiers and Modal Verbs

Zwiers (2008) reminds us that nuances of meaning can be conveyed by modal verbs and qualifiers, and that such nuances are often problematic for EL students. Take, for example, *often, only, usually*, and similar adverbs. We may think that we use such modifiers extensively in conversation. We do, but in academic texts they may not be used in the same way. There are also modifiers we do use more commonly in oral language, such as *just* and *nearly*. Students are well aware of how modifiers work in their oral language, but it is appropriate to draw their attention to their use in academic text, especially when they are engaged in searching the Internet for information or are engaged in Web searches.

Another way that nuances of meaning are conveyed is through modal verbs—for example, *could, would, may, must*. Authors use modals to signal, for example, *intent, obligation, possibility*, and *conditionality*. The modal *would* is often used in conditional statements, such as *If . . . would*. This form asks students to think about cause and effect. All the content areas ask students to employ this kind of thinking. Below, we talk about using frames such as *If . . . would* to develop students' understanding through discussion.

HOW CAN WE PROMOTE ACADEMIC LANGUAGE LEARNING?

Two important ways to develop academic language are through language analysis and through the use of frames. In this section, we describe the two approaches and include some related pedagogy.

Language Analysis

We have described how language can be analyzed at different levels: the word or lexical level, the grammatical level (sentence features, passive voice, and nominalization), and the discourse level (macro- and microstructures). Each of these levels of analysis can be introduced to the students through examples.

Once students have learned some of the language structures they may encounter in text, it may be appropriate to engage in a think-aloud to demonstrate how the structures work together to provide meaning. Too often, in our experience, teachers may engage in thinking aloud, and the students sit there looking puzzled because they have no idea what they are supposed to be observing. One way around this is to provide them with a way of marking the text. Using color-coded sticky notes or tabs is an easy way of doing this. The chart in Figure 2.3 gives an example.

The teacher reads a segment of the text aloud, stopping at various points to think aloud about the text structures as they occur. When the students hear the name of a structure, they put the appropriate-colored note or tab in their text. Students may initially need prompting to fully understand the task. Once they have done so, the students can engage in a think–pair–share, where they mark their texts individually, then meet with a partner to compare their markings. They might make a bar chart showing the number of structures that they have identified in a passage. This is a good way of showing students which structures are used most, and reminding them of all the ways they can engage effectively with text.

Text Structure	Color
Comparison	Green
Definition	Blue
Description	Red
Enumeration	Yellow
Exemplification	Purple
Explanation	Orange
Sequence	Aqua

FIGURE 2.3. Think-aloud color code.

Here is an example of a think-aloud using an excerpt from a sixth-grade science text. The text reads:

Angiosperms

Most of the plants that live on earth are angiosperms. Angiosperms produce seeds from flowers, and all produce some kind of fruit. Crop plants, hardwood trees, shrubs, grasses, and desert plants are all angiosperms. Angiosperms are divided into two groups: *dicots* and *monocots*. . . .

The vascular tissue bundles are arranged differently in dicots and monocots. In dicots, they are arranged in a circle. In monocots, vascular bundles are found throughout the stem. The leaves of the dicots are broad and have veins branching through them. Monocots have long leaves, and have veins that run from one end of the leaf to the other. Dicots include oaks, maples, elms, roses, beans, cabbages, tomatoes, and petunias. Monocots include grasses, palms, daffodils, irises, and lilies. (Watkins & Leto, 1994, p. 265)

The teacher's think-aloud may go something like this (the text as read aloud by the teacher is in italics):

Angiosperms. Most of the plants that live on earth are angiosperms. This sounds like the text is going to be a description of what angiosperms are. The author is starting with an example.—So, everyone, have you labeled this description and exemplification? OK. Keep marking your text.

Angiosperms produce seeds from flowers, and all produce some kind of fruit. This looks like a definition of what angiosperms are—plants that have flowers, seeds, and fruit.

Crop plants, hardwood trees, shrubs, grasses, and desert plants are all angiosperms. OK, here the author is giving us examples of angiosperms.

Angiosperms are divided into two groups: dicots and monocots. Mmm, the description is continuing with the author telling us there are two groups, so I am expecting a comparison structure. Let's see . . .

The vascular tissue bundles are arranged differently in dicots and monocots. In dicots, they are arranged in a circle. In monocots, vascular bundles are found throughout the stem. OK, here is the comparison: The vascular bundles are arranged differently.

The leaves of the dicots are broad and have veins branching through them. Monocots have long leaves, and have veins that run from one end of the leaf to the other. More comparison. So dicots and monocots have different types of leaves.

Dicots include oaks, maples, elms, roses, beans, cabbages, tomatoes, and petunias. Monocots include grasses, palms, daffodils, irises, and lilies. Oh, here are some examples of each type. So we have exemplification within a comparison structure. I can understand this better with these examples, as I think of the difference between a palm tree leaf and a maple leaf.

Different texts would need to be used to demonstrate all the structures. It is important for students to recognize that knowing which structures an author is using helps with understanding the text. This think-aloud and its extension into a think–pair–share provide an example of how modeling and discussion can help students analyze text structures. A similar process could occur with grammatical features, to teach students about sentence features, passive voice, nominalization, and modifiers/modals.

Teaching students to identify macrostructures can be accomplished through the use of graphic organizers, like those in Figure 2.1, applied to exemplar texts. Once again, modeling and discussion can be used to develop students' understanding. Some teachers also use these graphics to help students organize their thinking prior to writing. In some ways, they are frames. In the next section, we look at similar frames in more detail.

Fisher and Frey (2010) suggest another way to use language analysis. They recommend making explicit for EL students the language purposes for a lesson, as well as content purposes. After surveying teachers of K–12 EL students in California, they developed a framework that examines purposes related to vocabulary, language structure, and language function. They looked at statements about what teachers said were the language purposes of their lessons. Examples of these language purpose statements from social studies included the following (Fisher & Frey, 2010, p. 323):

Vocabulary—Name the routes and explorers on a map.

Language Structure—Sequence the steps of food production using the signal words *first, then, next,* and *finally.*

Language Function—Justify in a paragraph the ways fire was used for hunting, cooking, and warmth by citing three examples.

Fisher and Frey found three types of language structure statements that the teachers in their survey used: (1) specific grammar and syntax rules that students should practice; (2) signal words that are common in academic English; and (3) sentence frames representing certain language structures. They did not specify which functions teachers reported using, but gave examples from other researchers, such as *analyze, compare, describe, observe, summarize, persuade, sequence,* and *evaluate.* Fisher and Frey concluded that their framework is suitable for providing purposes in lessons for EL students. We think that they are probably suitable for all students.

Using Sentence Frames

The use of language frames that exemplify particular language patterns has been recommended in relation to students writing in elementary schools (Wray, 2001), but is now being suggested for use with students' oral language (Fisher & Frey, 2010). Frames can take a variety of forms. Carrier and Tatum (2006) extend the idea of word walls to using sentence walls. They argue that for EL students, "sentence walls provide a visual scaffold of language (e.g. phrases, sentences) to help students communicate in classroom discussions about content" (p. 286). They suggest that frames can be posted on classroom walls for students to refer to when talking about content. For example, question frames might include the following:

> What happens when . . . ?
> How does . . . ?
> What causes . . . to . . . ?

Carrier and Tatum also suggest sentence frames about specific content for statements to use in discussion—a type of sentence completion task.

> Snow falls when water . . .
> When water evaporates, it . . .
> Monocots have . . . , while dicots have . . .

They further recommend that sentence frames such as these should be linked to key vocabulary as part of a content-focused word wall.

Donnelly and Roe (2010) suggest three levels of sentence frames for developing students' understanding of academic language. They recommend that structures such as comparison–contrast be introduced by first presenting and comparing two simple sentences, then moving to a comparative sentence, and finally presenting a complex comparative sentence. For example, these two simple sentences might be used:

> A triangle has three sides. A quadrilateral has four sides. (_____
>   has _____.)

A comparative sentence might be this:

> Triangles and quadrilaterals are both plane figures, but triangles have three sides and quadrilaterals have four sides. (_____ and _____ are both _____, but _____ have _____ and _____ have _____.)

A complex comparative sentence might be this:

> The main difference between triangles and quadrilaterals is that triangles have three sides, while quadrilaterals have four sides. (The main difference between _____ and _____ is that _____ have _____, while _____ have _____.)

Donnelly and Roe (2010) recommend introducing such frames through modeling, group practice, and then individual application.

Ross, Fisher, and Frey (2009, p. 29) developed six categories of sentence frames for argumentation in science, with examples of frames for students to use in each category:

> *Making a claim.* I noticed . . . when . . . ; I compared . . . and . . .
>
> *Providing evidence.* I know that . . . is . . . because . . . ; Based on . . . , I think . . .
>
> *Asking for evidence.* I have a question about . . . ; What causes . . . to . . . ?
>
> *Offering a counterclaim.* I disagree with . . . because . . . ; In my opinion . . .
>
> *Inviting speculation.* I wonder what would happen if . . . ; We want to test . . . to find out if . . .
>
> *Reaching consensus.* I agree with . . . because . . .

These frames are designed to be used in conversation, and only some are included here. For the full list, we refer you to the original Ross and colleagues (2009) article. Later in this book, we suggest the use of sentence frames as part of Partner Reading and Content, Too (PRC2) and other discussion routines.

CONCLUDING THOUGHTS

In this age of new literacies (Baker, 2010), we need to consider that students will be engaging with multimedia texts. These multisemiotic texts make meaning in a variety of ways that go beyond traditional written texts, and we will have to consider the many ways that they make meaning in the content areas. Sentence and text structure, grammars and rhetorical structures, may be only part of what we need to teach students. In fact, even the ways in which we teach students about academic language will be influenced by digital media and other forms of new literacies. This is an exciting and yet complex time, in which our students may be teaching us about some texts as we teach them about others.

DISCUSSION QUESTIONS

1. Review the concept of a language register. Think of times when you use different language registers in your class. Are you aware of doing so? Do you think your students would benefit from being told about when this happens and why?

2. The CCSS ask us to use complex texts. How might complex sentence structures lead to confusion for some students? Can you think of examples of when this has happened in your classroom? What can you do to teach students about such structures?

3. Write a paragraph that uses nominalization as a cohesive device. How easy or difficult was this? Could you teach your students to do this? How else might you introduce them to nominalization and how it works in academic language?

CHAPTER 3 ▨▨▨▨▨▨▨▨▨▨▨▨▨▨▨▨▨

Understanding Effective
Vocabulary Instruction

Notes from a teacher study group on responses to the question "Where do we go next?":

> JESSE: I am getting really confused by all these vocabulary strategies. I feel like I have a cookbook, but no plan about what to cook when.
>
> MARTA: I want to have a better idea of how to organize all this in my day, my week, my units, my year. What fits where?
>
> HUGH: Now the big push is for academic vocabulary, but I don't feel like I have regular vocabulary under control. *Is* there "regular" vocabulary?

In the preceding chapters, we have introduced you to ideas and questions about academic vocabulary and academic language. As a bridge to the rest of this book, which focuses on instruction in specific content domains, this chapter provides you with an overview of what educational researchers and practitioners know and think about effective general vocabulary instruction. If you already know a lot about this topic, you might want to skim the headings in this chapter to see where you want to focus. If you are a newcomer to thinking about vocabulary instruction, this chapter will help you build background. We start with a brief overview of some of the key research, resulting in four basic understandings that underpin good vocabulary instruction. We follow this with a description of the four essential components of comprehensive vocabulary instruction and the roles of key players—parents, the school, and the principal, as well as teachers and students.

THE BACKGROUND BUILDERS

The last two decades have seen an explosion of interest in vocabulary instruction—an interest that builds on years of research and practical experimentation. If you are interested in building your background in this research, the second volume of the *Handbook of Reading Research* (Barr, Kamil, Mosenthal, & Pearson, 1991) contains two foundational chapters on vocabulary: one dealing with vocabulary processes (Anderson & Nagy, 1991) and a second with vocabulary development (Beck & McKeown, 1991). These same two topics were updated in chapters (Blachowicz & Fisher, 2000; Nagy & Scott, 2000) in the subsequent third volume of the handbook, as well as in a chapter of the *Handbook of Teaching the English Language Arts* (Baumann, Kame'enui, & Ash, 2003) and in another comprehensive volume (Farstrup & Samuels, 2008).

Happily, literacy educators have surveyed this landscape of research and attempted to interpret it for practitioners in research-based application volumes focused on instruction (Beck et al., 2013; Blachowicz & Fisher, 2010; Frey & Fisher, 2009; Graves, 2006; Hiebert & Kamil, 2005; Kame'enui & Baumann, 2012; Lubliner & Scott, 2008). There are also many short and specific articles that present overviews of the landscape. Key facets of study have included the nature of vocabulary acquisition, including the wide array of information needed for truly "knowing" a word (Nagy, Herman, & Anderson, 1985); characteristics associated with effective instruction of individual word meanings (Mezynski, 1983; Stahl & Fairbanks, 1986); strategies that individuals use to determine the meanings of unknown words encountered in reading and the ways they can be successfully taught (Baumann, Edwards, Boland, Olejnik, & Kame'enui, 2003); and characteristics of and differences in vocabulary acquisition across students (Biemiller & Slonim, 2001; Hart & Risley, 1995).

The practical implication of all this information is that in order to address the complex, multidimensional nature of word learning, we need to approach vocabulary comprehensively (Stahl & Nagy, 2006; Watts Taffe, Fisher, & Blachowicz, 2009).

This leads us to some key concepts that are critical to structuring good instruction.

FOUR BASIC UNDERSTANDINGS

Four things that flow out of this research are "basics" to understanding good vocabulary instruction:

- The term *vocabulary* has multiple meanings.
- Vocabulary learning is incremental.
- Vocabulary learning is both incidental and intentional.
- Vocabulary instruction is *everyone's* responsibility.

The Term *Vocabulary* Has Multiple Meanings

Everyone has many types of "vocabularies." We have already introduced the idea that academic vocabulary is a special kind of vocabulary, and this idea is well developed in the following chapters. When we use the term *vocabulary*, sometimes we are talking about the words that students use in speech (oral vocabulary) but are not yet able to decode in written text (reading vocabulary). Sometimes they can understand a word they hear (listening vocabulary) but cannot use that same word in speech or writing. Figure 3.1 shows a handy way of organizing what we know about types of vocabulary.

Students' receptive vocabularies are often far more advanced than their expressive ones, especially in the early grades. In fact, Biemiller and Slonim (2001) propose that students' receptive vocabularies can be at least two grade levels higher than their expressive vocabularies. So when we read to children, we can use more difficult vocabulary to stretch their receptive abilities. Expressive use of words is often considered more difficult than receptive use. For reading or listening, students often just need a general idea of a word and can use syntactic and semantic context clues to help them understand; to use it in speech or writing, more precision is required in both meaning and usage. In school, we want to develop all four of these areas: oral receptive vocabulary (for listening), oral expressive vocabulary (for speaking), reading (receptive) vocabulary, and writing (expressive) vocabulary.

Vocabulary Learning Is Incremental

Most researchers agree that word learning is not an all-or-nothing proposition, like a switch that turns a light on or off. A better metaphor is that of a dimmer switch, which gradually supplies an increasingly rich supply of light. For example,

	Receptive	Expressive
Oral	Listening	Speaking
Written	Reading	Writing

FIGURE 3.1. We all have different types of vocabularies.

children learn the word *daddy, papi*, or *papa* and begin to apply it to all men, sometimes with humorous results. Ultimately they narrow its meaning to their own fathers or learn to use it with qualifications, such as "Maria's *papi*." This commonly observed process mirrors research suggesting that learners move from not knowing a word, to being somewhat acquainted with it, to a deeper, richer, more flexible word knowledge that allows them to use new words in many modalities of expression (Graves, 1986; McKeown & Beck, 1988). Repeated encounters with words in a variety of rich oral and written contexts provide experiences and clues to the words' meanings and limitations that build over time, helping to develop and change learners' mental structures for the words' meanings (Eller, Pappas, & Brown, 1988; Vosniadou & Ortony, 1983). Meaningful use, review, and practice that calls upon students to use vocabulary in authentic ways are all essential for developing rich and full word knowledge.

Vocabulary Learning Is Both Incidental and Intentional

Rich exposure to words, such as that provided by wide reading, helps students construct and retain meaningful personal contexts for words (Whittlesea, 1987). For example, reading the word *wardrobe* in *The Lion, the Witch and the Wardrobe* (Lewis, 1950) makes it meaningful in a way that a dictionary definition or an isolated sentence never could. Specific events in the novel help the learner note that a *wardrobe* is a piece of furniture, that it can be located in a bedroom, that it has a front door, and that it is big enough for a child to sit in and walk through. Readers who have read that wonderful book have no trouble conceptualizing or remembering the term *wardrobe*.

Estimates suggest that school-age children learn an average of 3,000-4,000 words per year (D'Anna, Zechmeister, & Hall, 1991; Nagy & Herman, 1987), although some researchers have suggested that this average varies widely, depending on students' background of home and school experiences (Becker, 1977; White, Graves, & Slater, 1990). The term *learning* in most of these studies refers to growth in familiarity of recognition for certain frequently encountered words, as measured on wide-scale tests or through research studies such as those carried out for *The Living Word Vocabulary* (Dale & O'Rourke, 1976). This rapid and large growth suggests that a significant amount of vocabulary learning takes place through incidental or environmental learning (including, e.g., wide reading, discussion, listening, and exposure to the mass media), rather than from direct instruction. For instance, students who know the word *sweeper* as a position in soccer have typically learned that through play and experience, not through books. Children learn from interacting with and using words in all sorts of meaningful contexts, and it is important for the classroom to support and build on this kind of learning.

But vocabulary can also be learned and taught intentionally, through explicit or implicit instruction. From the popularity of *Reader's Digest* "How to Increase Your Word Power" exercises in the 1950s and 1960s, to the executive word power programs advertised in airline magazines, deliberate study has always been part of adult self-improvement models. For school-age children, research suggests that the intentional teaching of specific words and word-learning strategies can build students' vocabularies (Lesaux et al., 2010; Tomeson & Aarnoutse, 1998), as well as improve reading comprehension of texts containing those words (see McKeown, Beck, Omanson, & Pople, 1985; Stahl & Fairbanks, 1986). For students whose heritage languages are not English, or those who struggle with reading, this instruction can be even more critical.

Vocabulary Instruction Is *Everyone's* Responsibility

A last basic understanding is the need for a schoolwide commitment to developing vocabulary. "We're all in this together" is a good slogan to describe school communities that know attention to vocabulary is an important part of their job. Parents and families, schools, and principals, as well as teachers and students, all have important parts to play in building strong vocabularies for school-age children.

Parents and Families

Parents' are our students' first teachers, and the role of parental input was highlighted by Hart and Risley's (1995) landmark study of preschool vocabulary learning. They found that children from homes with less frequent talk had a significantly smaller number of words in their oral vocabularies when they entered school. Graves (1986) has suggested that the gap in kindergarten between the most and least verbally advantaged students is about 3,000 words. These studies clearly demonstrate the importance of parent–child talk—both in frequency and in the number of words to which parents expose their children—for vocabulary learning.

The School

Schools cannot redo a child's preschool experiences, but they can support parents in moving their children forward. Family reading nights with ideas for parents, sending home books for home reading (and tapes or CDs for listening when homes have limited readers available), word play games and ideas are all supports for parents to engage their children in talk and book language. One elementary school we work with has a circulating library of word games (see Chapter 8 for examples) and joke and riddle books, and encourages parents to borrow these for home play. Other schools collaborate with local reading councils to prepare book bags for home or summer reading, choosing books with stimulating vocabulary. This reflects what we know about independent reading as a stimulant for vocabulary growth.

The school librarian can also assist in the task of locating games and books in the heritage languages of the school's students. For example, Scrabble has a new Scrabble Junior game featuring Dora the Explorer; the game board is two-sided, with English on one side and Spanish on the other. All these home–school collaborations can support parents in being the best first teachers they all want to be, and in participating with their children in playful vocabulary activities.

The Principal

Education research has firmly established that the principal is a key collaborator in motivating teachers, implementing a solid curriculum, and maintaining a positive school environment (Institute for Educational Leadership, 2000); this is something teachers and parents all understand. Just as "one-shot" professional development has limited impact, so too do "one-teacher, one-year" vocabulary programs. The whole school needs to acknowledge the importance of building vocabularies and work together to make this an emphasis across the grades.

The principal affects this, first of all, by engaging a school's teachers in professional development and study groups to build their content knowledge about good vocabulary instruction. There is an abundance of support materials for such study, including the teacher-focused resources we have mentioned above (see "The Background Builders"); materials specifically designed for study groups (Dimino & Taylor, 2009; Graves, 2009); and "action packs" for teachers and coaches (Blachowicz & Cobb, 2007), which share specific ideas for curricular improvement.

Besides planning focused and ongoing staff development in vocabulary instruction, the principal's best role is as "cheerleader" for vocabulary. Finding ways to highlight vocabulary and have fun with words as a whole school can help everyone—students, teachers, and parents—become enthusiastic. Washington School, in Evanston, Illinois, has added vocabulary to Halloween by having students include a vocabulary word in their costume that relates to their costume. Figure 3.2 shows a hot dog of a teacher (a nice *plump* hot dog) with a *ghoulish* student; their enjoyment of this schoolwide activity is evident. Other ideas utilized in this school are having students post vocabulary words for the week in appropriate places in the school, and include vocabulary in their reporting of current happenings.

FIGURE 3.2. A teacher and student enjoying a schoolwide Halloween vocabulary activity.

The principal also needs to make sure that teachers across the school have the resources they need both to stimulate interest in words and to teach new vocabulary. The obvious resources are dictionaries, including "learner" dictionaries, games, books, and puzzle software, but creative use of other resources can be enormously helpful. For instance, one principal bought small whiteboards for each classroom. On the whiteboards, each class posted a few words it was studying each week, and trips down the halls became learning experiences for students. When one group of students passed another group on the way to lunch or gym, they could ask about any words they saw.

The principal also has a great tool for stimulating word learning: the public address system. Haggard (1982), in a study of word learning among middle school students, was perplexed by the fact that middle schoolers in one school all knew the meaning of the word *behoove*—not a common word even in most adults' vocabularies! She traced the learning back to the day before winter break, when the principal announced, "It behooves everyone to clean out his or her locker before the break. Things left in lockers will be thrown away." The students thought that *behoove* was one of the funniest words they had ever heard. That week, the teacher heard "It behooves you to get your feet off my chair," and "It behooves you to give me back my pencil." Funny-sounding words intrigue students.

In a more intentional way, one principal has students from one classroom each week announce four "special" words they are studying each Monday. The students post these four words in four public places in the school. For example, one week the word *informative* was posted on the library door, *perspire* in the gym, *selection* on the vending machine, and *linoleum* on the floor by the office. A manila folder was placed on the classroom door, and students could drop in their ideas about why certain words were in certain places. On Friday, the students would explain their reasoning about word placement and draw one idea out of the envelope. If the student drawn had an appropriate explanation, he or she received a ticket that entitled the student to certain school benefits. Besides providing good professional development and resources to teachers, the principal can do a great deal to highlight vocabulary learning and use as an all-school goal.

Teachers and students are at the heart of this process, and we examine their contributions and actions as we discuss what a comprehensive program looks like.

THE COMPREHENSIVE VOCABULARY PROGRAM

The diagram in Figure 3.3 can orient you to the components of a comprehensive vocabulary program (Baumann et al., 2011; Blachowicz & Baumann, 2013; Graves, 2006). We now discuss each of these components: (1) Providing rich and varied language experiences; (2) teaching specific vocabulary intentionally; (3) teaching word-learning strategies; and (4) fostering word consciousness.

Providing Rich and Varied Language Experiences

James Britton (1993) has noted, "Reading and writing float on a sea of language." This wonderful comment gives us a great visual metaphor for thinking about the first component of a comprehensive vocabulary program. In Figure 3.3, you can see that this "sea" of language surrounds everything else we do in vocabulary teaching.

We know that students learn words incidentally by reading independently (Cunningham, 2005; Kim & White, 2008; Swanborn & de Glopper, 1999), by listening to texts read aloud, and through exposure to enriched oral language (Dickinson & Smith, 1994). We know that students acquire vocabulary in an accelerated fashion through read-alouds when teachers or caregivers provide elaboration (definitional and contextual information) on words in the texts (Blachowicz & Obrochta, 2007; Bus, van IJzendoorn, & Pellegrini, 1995; van Kleeck, Stahl, & Bauer, 2003).

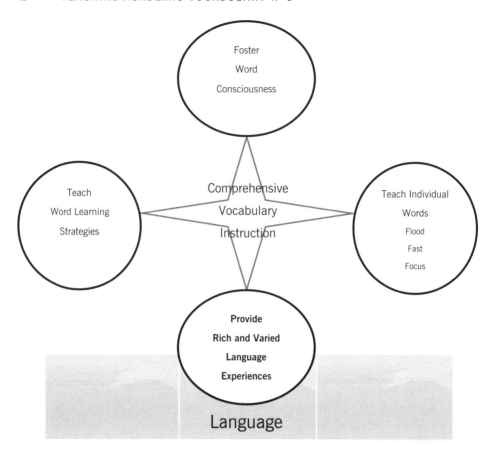

FIGURE 3.3. The four essential components of a comprehensive vocabulary program.

Thus we include in this component interactive read-aloud experiences, with teachers supporting and probing students' knowledge and word explanations (Beck et al., 2013; Biemiller & Boote, 2006) to promote students' learning and retention of new words.

What's in this "sea"? It's the environment in which word learning takes place. Teachers need to:

- Provide time to read aloud from stimulating texts with rich vocabulary. These read-alouds can be from materials that students would not be able to read themselves, but that they can understand. The activities should include discussion in which carefully chosen vocabulary can be highlighted during or after reading.
- Ensure time and support for regular personal reading of on-level texts. Teachers can model book selection and do book talks to stimulate interest in different genres, authors, and formats (electronic texts, manga, etc.).

- Provide time and support for meaningful student discussion and writing. Many students need to receive modeling and support for *how* to talk about a text or issue (Evans, 2002). This support may be as basic as taking turns, looking at the speaker, and giving some sort of response; or it may be more elaborate, such as the use of PRC2 (Ogle & Correa-Kovtun, 2010), discussion frames (Blachowicz, Bates, & Cieply, 2011), or charting for character traits (Manyak, 2007). We elaborate on these instructional approaches in later chapters. Similarly, in their writing, students need to be supported with graphics, planning, and other models to begin using elaborated vocabulary.

Teaching Individual Words

Students deserve to receive specific and intentional instruction on words that they need for successful participation in home, school, and community reading and writing. Words often encountered are referred to as *high-frequency* or *high-utility*. More school-centered vocabulary is the academic vocabulary that is our focus in the rest of this book. As we have noted earlier, this can be vocabulary that reflects general school tasks (e.g., *summarize*); or it might be focused on a particular content area, such as math (*diameter*), social studies (*Confederacy*), science (*photosynthesis*), literature (*genre*), or the arts (*Expressionism*). There are also domains of student interest that have specific vocabularies all their own, such as basketball (*cager*), snowboarding (*boogie board*), graphic reading materials (*manga*), yoga (*bikram*), gaming (*nerf*, and it's not a ball!), and so forth.

In planning for intentional instruction, teachers need to choose whether a word can be taught easily or whether it needs more intense instruction. Imagine a group of fourth-grade students who are well familiar with the word *crown*. Teaching the meaning of the word *diadem* won't be too difficult. They already have the concept of a crown and are learning only a new label for a related term. Little if any instruction might be needed, although repetition through reading and use can help the word "stick." For the same students in the same selection, however, the word *nostalgia* would probably be harder to teach. This is an abstract concept that might not be too familiar to most 9-year-olds, and the teacher would have to help the students establish a rich network of related concepts, such as longing, the past, and so forth. So it makes sense to look at "knowing" a word as a continuous process that can be affected by meaningful encounters with words and by instruction aimed at helping the learners develop a network of understanding. The instructional situation that the teacher selects will vary, depending both on the frameworks of knowledge the learners already have and the importance of the term to the task at hand.

General Instructional Framework for Teaching Individual Words

There are many different ways to teach individual words, but teachers need to make sure that students:

1. Hear and see, hear and say the word. Pronunciation can call up oral vocabulary if students know the word in speech.
2. Hear the word in context (usage and meaning).
3. Get to a definition. Teachers can elicit definitions from students and restate them or or provide a "kid-friendly" definition.
4. Make a personal connection and use the word in a meaningful way
5. Participate in a semantic decision task and explain reasoning. (Note that 4 and 5 can be done in reverse order.)
6. Record. This can be independent work in a vocabulary notebook, such as constructing a "four-square" for each vocabulary word (with the word in one square, a definition in the second, an example in the third, and a picture as a visual clue in the fourth square).

It's essential for students to revisit the words later in the lesson, and to continue encountering them in print and discussion, reading, research, inquiry, and writing.

Let's see what this looks like if a teacher wants to teach the meaning of *buffet* (meaning "to hit repeatedly"). First, the word is placed on the board, and the teacher leads the students through the steps:

1. "Let's say it . . . it's not boo/fay, it's buff/it." (See/say.)
2. "Here's an example. When there is a windstorm, the tree branches buffet my roof and knock off shingles." (Hear the word in context.)
3. "What could it mean?" (Get to a definition.) The teacher elicits or gives or restates a meaning: "Right, it means 'hit.'" The teacher then says, "Let's check," and has students give/find definition to confirm (optional if time).
4. "Turn and talk with your partner, and use *buffet* in a sentence about something you remember or imagine." (Make a personal connection.) The teacher can then give feedback on usage.
5. "Let me ask you a question. Would I want you to buffet others in the classroom? Why or why not?" (Participate in a decision task and explain reasoning.)
6. "OK, record *buffet* in your word book/sheet, and add a synonym or short definition and a picture that helps you remember the meaning." (Record.) The teacher can use this as meaningful seatwork or homework.

These steps are negotiable and can be organized according to what the students already know, but they will help establish a basic routine for teaching individual words.

Teaching Word-Learning Strategies

Students need to be able to strategically use context, as well as prefixes, suffixes, and roots, to infer the meanings of new words. This requires them to learn the meanings of prefixes and suffixes, and to engage in strategies for applying these generative elements to new words. They should also learn to use context clues when encountering unknown words (Baumann, Edwards, et al., 2003; Baumann, Ware, & Edwards, 2007; Fukkink & de Glopper, 1998). We deal with this extensively in Chapter 6, as well as throughout this book in each domain-focused chapter.

Fostering Word Consciousness

If the prior three components are being approached in an engaging manner, we teachers will have a head start on developing students' *word consciousness* (sometimes called *word awareness*)—that is, their understanding of how words work and their flexibility in using words (Graves, 2006; Nagy, 2005; Scott et al., 2012). We need to nurture our students' interest in words and their meanings, along with an appreciation of how writers and speakers choose and use specific words and phrases to convey different shades of meaning. We want them to have a playful and joyful pleasure in an interesting word or turn of phrase, and to appreciate the many ways they can use our rich and flexible language in their own speech and writing. The teacher self-evaluation checklist in Figure 3.4 highlights some of the important aspects of this component, many of which we develop in subsequent chapters. Some highlights of this checklist are discussed below.

- *Classroom environment*. The environment for word learning must be engaging. Having word games, books, puzzle-making software, and time to use all these will help students become word lovers. Word walls, student work, and other displays also emphasize that vocabulary learning is fun and important. Along with time devoted to reading and writing as described earlier, time for play is important.
- *Materials*. Besides playful materials, having a selection of different dictionaries (including topical ones, e.g., *Dictionary of Dance, The Automobile Dictionary*) and electronic resources makes it easy for students to pursue words

1. _____ **I show enthusiasm for words and word learning**

     _____ Daily read-aloud

     _____ Daily playful word activity

     _____ Students indicate *love* of words and word play

     _____ Understands differences and connections between spelling, phonics, and vocabulary

2. _____ **My classroom shows physical signs of word awareness**

     _____ Word charts or word walls (showing student input) used and changed regularly

     _____ Books on words, word play, specialized and learner dictionaries, dictionaries (where students can easily access them)

     _____ Labels in classroom

     _____ Word games

     _____ Puzzle books and software

     _____ Student made word books, alphabet books, dictionaries, computer files, PowerPoints, smartboard lessons

3. _____ **My students show enthusiasm for words and word learning**

     _____ Have personal dictionaries or word logs

     _____ Can use dictionary on appropriate level

     _____ Have a strategy for dealing with unknown words

     _____ Spend part of each day reading on appropriate level

     _____ Can name a favorite word book, puzzle activity, and/or word game

     _____ Use new vocabulary in talk, discussion, writing, and presentation

     _____ Enjoy and share new words, word games, word play

4. _____ **My vocabulary instruction includes**

     _____ Rich instruction on content-area vocabulary words with definitional and contextual information and usage in talk and writing

     _____ Use of mapping, webbing, and other graphics to show word relationships

     _____ Multiple exposures and chances to see, hear, write, and use new words

     _____ Wide reading with post-reading discussion of new words

     _____ Developing student's responsibility for self-selection and self-study by keeping of a word log

     _____ Teaching and practicing of independent strategies (word parts, context, and word references)

     _____ Word play and motivation activities

     _____ Engaging review and use in speaking, writing, discussion, and presentation

     _____ Varied assessments

5. _____ **Our school context for word learning**

     _____ Use of PA and other all-school communication for word consciousness

     _____ Visible schoolwide attention and appreciation of new words (e.g., school newspaper, bulletin boards, newsletters)

     _____ Supportive materials in all classrooms, libraries, and resource centers

     _____ Teacher study groups and sharing of vocabulary ideas

FIGURE 3.4. Teacher self-evaluation checklist.

related to their various interests. Also, learner dictionaries—those meant for students who have heritage languages other than English (e.g., the Longman Learner Dictionaries)—are essential for every classroom. See Chapter 8 for a full discussion of materials.

• *Models*. Students need to hear and read models of good language use. Teachers themselves, of course, are powerful models of spoken language, and videos of many eloquent public speakers reading to children are accessible today. The Rev. Jesse Jackson reading Dr. Seuss's (1960) *Green Eggs and Ham* (*www. youtube.com/watch?v=DPy2alWEZ-U*) is a favorite with students, and YouTube makes many other powerful speakers available to the classroom.

Books used as mentor texts for student writing and as models of fine word choice abound, from the works of Kevin Henkes in the early grades to those of Rick Riordan and J. K. Rowling for older students. Cunningham and Stanovich (1998) point out that even primary-level books have a more elevated level of vocabulary than the language most college-educated adults use in daily life.

Scott and colleagues (2012) have developed methods for discussing authors' language use in ways that influence student writing. Their Gifts of Words model engages students in selecting and sharing fine language use throughout the year and incorporating ideas into their own writing.

• Introducing word relationships. Every curriculum introduces the basic relationships of words as synonyms and words as antonyms. Understanding these two key relationships is a good starting point for becoming familiar with the ways words relate to one another. But there are many more relationships that form the foundation of an educated person's vocabulary. For example, the Wordle (*www. wordle.net*), or graphic "word cloud," shown in Figure 3.5 was made by students listing their favorite word relationships.

In short, students develop word consciousness by engaging in playful language activities; by making visual representations of categories, webs, and maps (such as the Wordle in Figure 3.5); and by exploring the words accomplished authors and speakers use (Graves & Watts-Taffe, 2002). Graphic mapping of complex word relationships, use of semantic organizers, word webs, word ladders, and the like make this learning concrete.

In our work in the schools, we have also learned the value of regular and engaging review (Blachowicz et al., 2011) in furthering our students' word consciousness. Revisiting both group and individual vocabulary in playful ways helps those words "stick" and encourages a lifelong interest in words, meanings, and ideas. For example, Connect Two (Blachowicz & Fisher, 2010; see Figure 3.6 on page 49) involves review that asks students to connect just two words from the weekly review list in a meaningful way.

FIGURE 3.5. A Wordle listing students' record of word relationships.

CONCLUDING THOUGHTS

In this chapter, we have rounded out your introduction to academic vocabulary, academic language, and comprehensive vocabulary instruction. This provides a foundation of background knowledge for your immersion in the more specific content-area chapters to follow.

DISCUSSION QUESTIONS

1. One of the four "basic understandings" presented in this chapter is that the term *vocabulary* is used in different ways to mean different things. Brainstorm with your group all the ways you have heard the term *vocabulary* used. Can you group these usages into similar usages? See whether Figure 3.1 on page 36 can help you. Explain your reasoning.

2. Discuss the statement "Vocabulary learning is incremental." Do you have, or can you imagine, any life experiences that provide examples of this statement? Your own? With children? Explain your examples.

3. Use Figure 3.4 on page 46 to reflect on your own teaching. Then critically evaluate on the checklist. What makes sense to you and why? What would you change and why? Work with your group to revise the checklist.

Connect Two Weekly Vocabulary Review Instructional Plan

Preparation time: 2–5 minutes

Classroom activity time: 5–10 minutes

Organization: Whole class/small groups/partners

Materials: Word wall weekly vocabulary chart

Procedure: Students choose two words from the word wall vocabulary chart that they believe belong together. The students must provide an explanation of why or how they believe the two words are connected. If their explanation makes sense and/or is reasonable, it is accepted. Students are encouraged to share connections orally or to use a template to respond in writing.

EXAMPLE

Word Wall Vocabulary Chart

consists	establish
roar	breath
fellow	journey
officer	roamed
ecosystem	relocate
disappear	factor
	product

CONNECTION (Meaning): *Factor* and *relocate* are connected because getting a new job could be a *factor* in needing to *relocate*.

CONNECTION (Word Feature): *Fellow* and *product* are connected because they both have two syllables. Emphasize meaning connections.

Connect Two Practice Sheet

Choose two words from your list. Describe how those two words are related.

_____ and _____

are connected because _____

_____.

_____ and _____

are connected because _____

_____.

_____ and _____

are connected because _____

_____.

_____ and _____

are connected because _____

_____.

_____ and _____

are connected because _____

_____.

FIGURE 3.6. Connect Two instructional plan and practice sheet. Based on International Reading Association (1986).

CHAPTER 4 ▰▰▰▰▰▰▰▰▰▰▰▰▰

Teaching Academic Vocabulary in the English Language Arts

I sat in a circle with one of my reading groups, a small group of four boys. They had just finished reading a book and were engaged in a lively discussion about it when I said, "Well, you boys are demonstrating excellent comprehension of this book." Jason raised his hand and asked, "What's comprehension?"
—SUSAN, DESCRIBING HER FIRST YEAR OF TEACHING

KEY UNDERSTANDINGS ABOUT ACADEMIC VOCABULARY IN READING AND WRITING

Unlike mathematics, science, social studies, and other "content areas," we tend to take for granted the academic language of the English language arts (ELA). After all, we begin using this type of language with children in preschool, and many parents begin using this language with their children even before then. Words like *read, story, picture, letter, word*, and *page* may feel natural in home and community settings, whereas "science words" such as *observe, experiment*, and *hypothesis* feel less like something to do at home and more like something to do at school. Twenty-first-century literacy "texts," such as those associated with the Internet, smartphones, and computer tablets, have increased the breadth of word knowledge young children are likely to acquire at home. Many children enter school knowing terms such as *click, download, link*, and *app*, which reflect literacy tools of the 21st century. It is a fact that children who enter school without the academic language and experiences associated with reading and writing are very often considered "at risk" for reading failure and are the recipients of "interventions." This is a testament to the degree to which this language and these experiences often go unconsidered in discussions of academic language in general. Yet, as Jason's question indicates, the words that are part of academic language in ELA are not automatically known to students.

"Literacy words" and "science words" are similar in that they are used to understand and communicate within their respective disciplines. In fact, these vocabulary words align with essential ways of thinking and being within each discipline. To hypothesize is to do more than understand the scientific process; to hypothesize is to *be* a scientist. To infer is to do more than understand the reading process; to infer is to *be* a reader. To plot the events in a story is to do more than understand the writing process; to do this is to *be* a writer. In this chapter, we focus on academic vocabulary pertinent to the content and processes of ELA.

We begin with a look at common features of ELA curricula and implications of the CCSS for academic vocabulary instruction in ELA. Then we consider approaches to teaching specific vocabulary for major strands within ELA: reading; writing; and listening and speaking. After considering ways to teach the meanings of specific words, we consider ways to approach word study, as well as strategies for independent word learning (such as structural analysis and contextual analysis). We conclude this chapter by discussing approaches to vocabulary assessment that can inform instruction in meaningful ways, and by providing resources for teachers to use as they bolster academic vocabulary instruction in ELA.

Throughout this chapter, you will find the elements of a comprehensive vocabulary program (discussed in Chapter 3) as applied to ELA. You will notice that these elements, like the strands within this disciplinary area itself, are not mutually exclusive and often intersect. As a reminder, these elements are as follows: (1) Provide rich and varied language experiences; (2) teach specific vocabulary intentionally; (3) teach word-learning strategies; and (4) foster word consciousness.

ELA CURRICULA

What Is Meant by ELA?

Traditionally, ELA curricula have included attention to reading, writing, speaking, and listening. The CCSS framework (NGA & CCSSO, 2010) delineates four overarching strands pertinent to these curricula: (1) reading (including literature, informational text, and foundational skills); (2) writing; (3) speaking and listening; and (4) language. The language strand includes standards specific to vocabulary acquisition and use, as well as general language competencies. However, it is clear that the CCSS call for the sophisticated use of language as an integral part of all curricular areas, not just the language strand.

A closer look at the reading, writing, and speaking–listening strands reveals important priorities for teaching and learning academic vocabulary in ELA. Table 4.1 illustrates the central role of academic vocabulary in the CCSS for ELA. For each of these three strands, a sample of academic vocabulary associated with the anchor standards is presented, in order to illustrate the kinds of words and concepts that elementary and middle school students will need to know and use in order to meet the CCSS requirements.

As readers and writers, students rely on the vocabulary shown in Table 4.1 as well as other related words in order to construct meaning. For example, predicting, summarizing, comparing, contrasting, inferencing, and evaluating are processes that readers engage in. As writers, students engage in outlining, explaining, supporting claims, describing scenes, adding details, developing characters, and creating mood. These academic words and the concepts they represent are important to *doing* reading and writing and, in essence, *being* readers and writers. Other academic vocabulary supports students in their abilities to respond to reading and writing. For our purposes, *responding* includes talking about, analyzing, critiquing, and evaluating. Here again, terms such as *character, setting, scene, plot, order of events, conflict*, and *resolution* are needed.

TABLE 4.1. Key Anchors of the CCSS and Associated Academic Vocabulary

Category of anchor standards	Sample of associated academic vocabulary for students to know
Reading literature strand	
Key ideas and details	*details, retell, central idea, summarize*
Craft and structure	*phrase, clause, punctuation, structure, beginning, conclusion, metaphor, drama, dialogue*
Integration of knowledge and ideas	*relationship, compare, contrast, mood*
Writing strand	
Text types and purposes	*opinion, narrative, informative, explanatory, transitional word, phrase*
Production and distribution	*planning, revising, editing, sequence, organizational structure, concluding statement*
Speaking and listening strand	
Comprehension and collaboration	*collaborate, explain, clarify, claim, evidence*
Presentation of knowledge and ideas	*report, main idea, details, fact, pace*

You will notice that the words and concepts in Table 4.1 include both general and domain-specific academic vocabulary. As discussed in Chapter 1 of this book, general academic vocabulary (i.e., words used across many academic contexts) will appear in domains other than ELA; such words are therefore ones to reinforce across content areas. Domain-specific words, on the other hand, are found in particular contexts and usually not found in other contexts. In Table 4.1, the words *summarize, clarify,* and *report* might be considered general academic vocabulary *and* domain-specific vocabulary. This is true for many words in ELA, since students will read, write, listen, and speak across academic domains. On the other hand, words like *punctuation, metaphor, narrative,* and *persuasive essay* are more specific to ELA. In this chapter, we focus on the academic vocabulary students use as they engage in reading, writing, listening, and speaking, and much of this vocabulary is also used in other domains.

How Are the ELA Strands Treated across the Grades?

Although there are differences in ELA curricula as students progress through the grades, the fundamental academic vocabulary of reading, writing, listening, and speaking is widely applicable. Over time, students increase their depth of knowledge related to these words and learn to apply them in increasingly sophisticated ways. Differences across the grades are more evident in approaches to instruction and allocation of time. A myriad of scheduling configurations for ELA, as well as a variety of instructional approaches, are used across school districts. In the primary grades, for example, reading and writing may be taught either separately or in a single, extended time block. Published materials of some kind are often a part of reading instruction, which may also include guided reading groups (Fountas & Pinnell, 1996). In addition, mechanisms are in place to encourage and support students as they engage in independent reading of self-selected books. Instruction in handwriting, grammar, and spelling may also be treated separately, or it may be integrated with writing instruction. Listening and speaking may not be considered as formal areas for instruction, but are very much understood to be a part of the primary-level curriculum (Jolongo, 2008; Strickland & Riley-Ayers, 2006).

In the upper elementary grades, there may be greater variation in the methods and materials used to teach reading. In some schools, published reading programs are used; in others, a reading workshop approach (Sarafini, 2001) is used; and in still others, a combination of the two is used. Independent reading takes on a larger role, and in some schools reading instruction includes a literature study component. In the middle grades, classes in literature tend to replace reading as a subject area, though some students will devote a portion of their day to reading and study skills. Writing may or may not be taught separately, but expectations for greater amounts of writing and for writing of a higher quality will be present across the school day.

The time spent on each of these areas varies widely across the nation, though it is safe to say that the greatest amounts of dedicated time for reading and writing occur in the primary grades, with less time spent in the upper elementary and middle grades to allow for greater attention to (and, ideally, integration of) reading and writing within other content areas. The instructional approaches discussed in this chapter have been selected with these differences in mind. They have been used successfully in a variety of settings and can be adapted to fit within multiple contexts. As you read, we encourage you to actively consider the ways in which these techniques can be incorporated into your setting.

TEACHING INDIVIDUAL DOMAIN-SPECIFIC WORDS

Selecting Words to Teach

Before we consider the specifics of teaching academic vocabulary to support reading, writing, listening, and speaking, we want to address the question of which words to teach. As shown in Table 4.2, several different types of words are required for academic success, and these words are used for specific purposes in ELA.

Selecting words for instruction in ELA can be a challenge. Some words are clearly "linchpin words" required for reading and writing across genres. These words, such as *main idea, sequence, context*, and *definition*, are used to describe and engage in the very processes of reading and writing, and so may be thought of as *process words*. Other words are *comprehension words* required to understand and describe a particular text, and it can be more difficult to decide which of these to teach. Although many are likely to come up in other texts, some words are more idiosyncratic.

In E. B. White's *Charlotte's Web* (1952), for example, the words *injustice, mercy, descended*, and *anxiety* are words students are likely to encounter in other texts. The words *runt, salutations*, and *spinnerets* will also be encountered elsewhere, though less frequently than the first set of words. Still, these words are important to understanding *Charlotte's Web*. In disciplines such as social studies and mathematics, comprehension words and concepts tend to be introduced and built upon across the length of the school year, contributing to a cumulative learning effect. But how often will students encounter the words needed to comprehend a piece of literature during the course of a school year? When teachers keep records of word selection, and plan ways to reinforce new words

TABLE 4.2. Important Types of Academic Vocabulary for Being Effective Readers and Writers

Important word types	Examples	Purposes for which these words are used
Comprehension process words	*compare, contrast, summarize, infer, main idea, supporting detail, sequence*	To describe and engage in the process of comprehension.
Vocabulary process words	*definition, association, context, root, prefix, glossary, thesaurus*	To describe and engage in the process of learning word meanings.
Writing process words	*brainstorm, rough draft, revise, edit, publish, cut, paste*	To describe and engage in the process of writing.
Craft words	*details, rich description, mood, tone, voice, personification, hyperbole, main point, facts, argument, evidence, details, rationale, persuasion*	To construct narrative or expository texts (e.g., fictional story, memoir, persuasive essay, biographical sketch). These words are also used to respond to, analyze, and critique texts that others have written.
Text structure words	Story grammar *narrative, character, traits, setting, plot, order of events, conflict, resolution* Informational text *topic sentence, supporting details, summary, comparison–contrast, enumeration, cause–effect*	To describe, respond to, and analyze various types of texts.
Character trait words	*brave, confident, patient, reliable, courageous, persistent, sensitive, trustworthy, hesitant*	To describe and respond to characters or real people in texts that students read and write.
Genre words	*realistic fiction, historical fiction, folktale, mystery, fantasy, nonfiction, biography, autobiography, poetry, play, film, blog, iMovie*	To describe genres for reading and writing, including newer mixed-media genres.
Figurative language	*missed the boat, right on target, pulling my leg, rub it in, a bird in the hand is worth two in the bush*	To describe and respond to characters or situations with language that is not to be taken literally.

over time and across the strands of reading, writing, listening, and speaking, the answer is more predictable, and student learning is bolstered. In some schools, collaborative teams work together to ensure meaningful, cohesive instruction in academic words that are deemed particularly important. Beck, McKeown, and Kucan (2002), Manyak (2007), Marzano and Pickering (2005), and Zwiers (2008) offer suggestions for various types of words that are important in ELA. We offer these general guidelines for word selection and instruction.

Process Words

Teach Them and Do Them. In the classroom excerpt that opens this chapter, Susan's students were clearly "doing" comprehension through literature discussion. However, at least one of her students didn't know the academic term *comprehension*. Without this knowledge, students like Jason are at a disadvantage whenever the term is used, and it is routinely used when students are required to demonstrate their understanding of what they have read. It is important to note, that we do not advocate teaching academic words that students will not use. For example, it would not be fruitful to teach a kindergartener the word *phoneme*, even though kindergarteners are taught to attend to them. However, for those terms that students will use, such as *comprehend* and *predict*, we advocate clearly teaching each term itself and then using it with students as they engage in the act represented by the term.

Comprehension Words

Select Words That Are Critical for Text Comprehension and Unknown to Students. Most of us do a good job of selecting words that are critical to understanding particular texts. However, we often forget that the importance of learning a new word is dictated not only by the text, but by the students who are reading the text. Existing word knowledge varies greatly among students (Graves, 2006), and words identified as "new" in published reading programs may or may not be new to your students. Conversely, words that are not identified as "new" may well be. Fortunately, research indicates that students can be taught to gauge their own word knowledge accurately (Blachowicz & Fisher, 2010; Harmon, Hedrick, Wood, & Gress, 2005), and that asking them to rate their knowledge before and after instruction increases their learning while promoting word consciousness. Knowledge rating charts (Blachowicz, 1987) like the one shown in Figure 4.1 can be completed individually or by a class.

Select Words That Are Useful, and Can Be Reinforced, in Other Contexts. Many words encountered in literature will come up in other contexts, helping to reinforce learning for students. However, it is also a good idea to insert and highlight new words intentionally in other contexts. Some teachers do this by keeping a weekly list of new words at their desks, as a reminder to use these words in conversation and point them out as they arise in other contexts. Others keep word lists on a bulletin board or ring chart, encouraging students to use these words in their writing and speaking, and to look for instances of these words across the week.

Before Reading

Word	1 Can Define and Use	2 Heard It Before	3 Don't Know
burly	✓		
subdued		✓	
pompous			✓
inquisitive		✓	
unique	✓		
warrant		✓	
expedition	✓		
belatedly		✓	
promenade			✓
strut		✓	

After Reading

Word	1 Can Define and Use	2 Heard It Before	3 Don't Know
burly	✓		
subdued		✓	
pompous	✓		
inquisitive	✓		
unique	✓		
warrant	✓		
expedition	✓		
belatedly	✓		
promenade	✓		
strut	✓		

FIGURE 4.1. Knowledge rating charts for words in *Mr. Popper's Penguins* (Atwater & Atwater, 1988).

Make Space in the Classroom for Words as They Are Being Learned. As noted previously, practice is much easier when both teachers and students are reminded to do it. By creating a space in the classroom for the growing bank of words students are acquiring, teachers can remind students to try these words in their writing and speaking, and to be on the lookout for these words in their reading and listening.

Once words for instruction have been identified—whether by the teacher, the students, recommendations in a published reading program, grade-level or buildingwide consensus on particular sets of words, or some combination of these—it is important to use instructional time wisely. We now turn to examples of instruction designed to promote in-depth, long-term learning. The examples are organized into three groups, covered in the next three sections: reading and responding to reading; writing and responding to writing; and listening and speaking. In this way, we hope to draw attention to the importance of teaching students not only how to read and write, but also how to respond to, analyze, and critique reading and writing. As we now sit squarely in the 21st century, it is imperative not only that students be able to read and write in order to understand and convey ideas, but also that they be equipped to respond to and evaluate what they read and write. As you read, remember that an example associated with vocabulary for reading can also be used to establish vocabulary for writing, as well as for listening and speaking. The most effective ELA instruction is integrated instruction (Gambrell, Malloy, & Mazzoni, 2011).

VOCABULARY INSTRUCTION FOR BEING A READER AND RESPONDING TO READING

Vocabulary Picture Walk

Taking a *picture walk* prior to reading is a great way to introduce a text selection. By previewing the illustrations, students can activate relevant prior knowledge and begin to think about, or even predict, what they may encounter in the text. Picture walks facilitate activation of relevant prior knowledge and engagement with the text. The *vocabulary picture walk* is a takeoff on this idea, with a focus on generating words and concepts that may be encountered during reading. As the teacher leads students through the pictures, he or she asks them to think of words that come to mind, especially in relation to the title or topic of the reading selection. If the book is short, all of the pictures may be shown. For longer books, we recommend selecting a handful of illustrations likely to elicit meaningful responses. Words are recorded and revisited after the reading. Whether the words or concepts are encountered in the story or not, this activity stimulates word consciousness specific to the text at hand, while simultaneously activating prior knowledge and occasionally shedding light on background knowledge the teacher might wish to build prior to reading.

Recently Mrs. Dooley took her first graders on a vocabulary picture walk for the selection "Alexander Graham Bell: A Great Inventor" (Blanton, 2011) found in her reading series. When her students previewed the illustrations, they came up with the following words: *child, piano, saw, workbench, test, drawing, dog, sick, illness, show, audience, telephone,* and *cell phone*. When the class returned to this list after reading, Mrs. Dooley asked whether her students could figure out why some of the words were shown in pictures, but not used in the text. A vocabulary picture walk among a small group of fourth graders reading *My Brother Martin: A Sister Remembers Growing Up with the Rev. Dr. Martin Luther King, Jr.* (Farris, 2003), yielded the following words in reference to this memoir: *joy, engrossed, frightened, prank, pranksters, playing, fire engine, sadness, pastor, sermon, preaching,* and *marches*. For older students, this technique can be used to help students engage quickly with a longer text.

Vocab-O-Grams

Vocab-o-Grams (Blachowicz & Fisher, 2010) are helpful for learning the meanings of words in stories. Prior to reading, and using story grammar elements as a guide, students work together to predict which words fit with which story grammar elements. Before reading *Balto and the Great Race* (Kimmel, 1999), based on the true story of a sled dog's important role in curbing the 1925 diphtheria outbreak in Nome, Alaska, third-grade teacher Mrs. Payne introduced the following words: *Alaska, endurance, frontier, mushers, rivalry, epidemic, diphtheria, isolated, urgent, sled dog, sled driver, transported, cargo.* She then had students work in triads to predict which words the author would use to describe characters, setting, problem, and actions in the story. After reading the first two chapters, the triads revisited their predictions and made adjustments based on their reading. Figure 4.2 shows one group's work. As reading progressed, the story grammar element of resolution was added, and the students returned to the rows for "problem or goal" and "resolution," since multiple subproblems were encountered in the reading.

Vocabulary Images

Associating new vocabulary with a visual aid, such as a drawing, a photograph, a gesture, an action, or simply the real thing, greatly enhances learning for all students and for ELs in particular. Sometimes this is easy to do, as in the case of a fourth-grade teacher who shared the meaning of the expression *circular file* by

Pre-Reading Vocab-o-Gram	
Use vocabulary to make predictions about . . . *(words may be used more than once)*	
Setting *Alaska, frontier, isolated*	**What might the setting be like?** *It might be far away from a big city.*
Characters *sled driver, sled dog, isolated*	**What do you think about the characters?** *There's a sled dog and a sled driver.* *The people might feel isolated.*
Problem or goal *rivalry, epidemic, urgent*	**What might it be?** *There might be a rivalry.* *There's an epidemic and people get sick.* *The problem is urgent.*
Actions *transported, endurance*	**What might happen?** *Somebody has to take something somewhere.* *Somebody has to have endurance.*
Resolution	**How might it end?**
What questions do you have? *Where is Alaska? Who's going to get sick first and start the epidemic?*	
Mystery words: *diphtheria, cargo, mushers*	

FIGURE 4.2. Vocab-o-Gram for Chapters 1 and 2 of *Balto and the Great Race.*

holding the classroom's garbage can out in front of her. When the real thing is not available, or when the word does not depict a "thing," vocabulary images provide a rich way for students to understand the meaning of a new word. Ms. Shelley found that a variety of images related to the word *shimmer* were far more powerful for her fifth graders than her explanation alone. She shared photographs to show various depictions of the word. Images such as these can be found online (or in magazines) and are free to share. Not only do they richly capture the word's meaning, but, taken together, they illustrate the core idea conveyed by the word while also showing variations in meaning. For example, Ms. Shelley's students came to understand that *shimmer* can refer to sunlight on water as well as glitter on paper. We work with teachers at all levels, primary through middle grades, who utilize images such as these in their instruction. Some teachers use presentation software such as PowerPoint to share the images "on the big screen"; others print the slides for students to use at school and at home; and still others involve students in the process of finding and sharing images, with different pairs or small groups responsible for presenting to the class sets of images associated with new words. (Note: When you are searching for images to reproduce, it is important to search for "free images," and when you are engaging students in online image searches, it is always important to adhere to the Internet safety protocol of your school.)

Read-Alouds

For a number of reasons, read-alouds are extremely important for teaching new words. Well-written books, read aloud, expose students to words they are unlikely to encounter in conversation and in books they can read independently, especially in the primary grades. Research indicates that even without instruction, students learn word meanings incidentally from read-alouds and other exposures to rich oral language (Christ, 2007; Elley, 1989). With repeated readings and intentional discussion of words found in read-alouds, the number of words learned increases dramatically, even for ELs who do not yet know a great deal of English (Beck & McKeown, 2007; Collins, 2010; van Kleeck, Stahl, & Bauer, 2003). Productive conversations about words include the characteristics of effective instruction discussed in Chapter 3: a student-friendly definition, contextual information going beyond the context provided by the read-aloud itself, and an opportunity for cognitive engagement with the word on the part of students. Based on Beck colleagues' (2002) work, Watts Taffe (2008) suggests "the 3 E's" as a mnemonic to support rich conversations about words: Explain (the meaning of the word), Extend (beyond the immediate context), and Engage (students with the word's meaning). Here is an example of the 3 E's at work in Miss Tracey's kindergarten classroom during a read-aloud of Maurice Sendak's *Where the Wild Things Are* (1963).

> MISS TRACEY: [reading aloud] "The night Max wore his wolf suit and made mischief of one kind and another, his mother called him "Wild Thing!" and Max said, 'I'll eat you up!,' so he was sent to bed without eating anything." Boys and girls, what do you think the author means when he says that Max made *mischief*?

> ALEX: He made trouble!

> MISS TRACEY: Very good, Alex. *Mischief* is another word for trouble or getting into something that you shouldn't. Remember our Curious George books? George is another character who makes mischief. Can you think of other characters we've read about who get into trouble, or make mischief?

> Maria: What about Owen with his blanket? Remember how he hid his blanket and put vinegar on it so his parents wouldn't take it away?

> SAM: No, no. He didn't put vinegar on it; his parents put vinegar on it so he wouldn't want it any more.

> MISS TRACEY: That's right. Good memory, guys. And then Owen rubbed his blanket all over the sandbox to get the vinegar smell out. His parents

probably thought he was getting into mischief when he did that. Do you think he thought he was getting into mischief?

SAM: No. Well, maybe.

MARIA: He just really wanted to keep his blanket.

MISS TRACEY: Yes, he did. Sometimes people know they are getting into mischief, and sometimes they don't. Looking at the pictures of Max in this book, it looks like he is playing make-believe—one of the things Owen liked to do with his blanket. But I'll bet his mother thought he was getting into mischief. Can you think of a time when you or someone you know has gotten into mischief?

CARA: My little sister, she's always in mischief. She's real little, and she's always doing things she shouldn't. That's why my mother can't leave her alone in a room. Someone's always gotta watch her.

MISS TRACEY: How old is your sister?

CARA: She's 2.

MISS TRACEY: Yes, 2-year-olds are known for getting into mischief, even though to them they are just exploring the world. But if someone doesn't watch them, they really can get into trouble.

This example makes it clear why discussion is such an important part of teaching word meanings. First, it allowed for an exchange of information between Miss Tracey and her students. Such an exchange is vital for students to make connections with their prior knowledge (linked with developing strong semantic relationships), since only they know what their prior knowledge is. While the entire class might recall an earlier encounter with Kevin Henkes's popular book *Owen* (1993), Cara made a personal connection with her toddler sister because she was given the opportunity to do so. Second, it allowed Miss Tracey to learn about possible misunderstandings and to clarify knowledge as needed. In this case, she helped her students to see that *mischief* is often the type of trouble someone gets into without meaning to, as is the case with Owen, Curious George, and Cara's sister. In Mrs. Axelrod's fifth-grade class, the words *tyrannical* and *traitors* were discussed in a similar fashion during a read-aloud of Avi's *The Fighting Ground* (1984).

Clearly, there are many ways to teach and reinforce vocabulary related to the processes of reading and responding to text. In the examples we've shared, the teachers successfully piqued curiosity about the text at hand, stimulated connections between new knowledge and prior knowledge, and fostered cognitive engagement with new concepts.

VOCABULARY INSTRUCTION FOR BEING A WRITER AND RESPONDING TO WRITING

There are different shades to words just like there are different shades
of paint and . . . they should be attempting to paint. You can't paint a
vivid picture when all you have are five crayons.
—MISS SMITH, FOURTH-GRADE TEACHER (cited in Watts, 1991, p. 142)

In our work with teachers, we have found that most feel more comfortable and
capable teaching reading than teaching writing. This may be in part because
reading tends to be the foremost component of the ELA curriculum; yet even in
kindergarten, the CCSS call for students to use drawing, dictating, and writing
to share opinions, inform and explain, narrate events, and react to events. With
an eye toward college and career readiness, the CCSS are clear on the need for
students to write regularly and "for a range of tasks, purposes, and audiences"
(NGO & CCSSO, 2010, p. 18). In this section, we share instructional approaches
that are aligned with these goals.

Language Frames

Language frames can be used to promote academic language learning, both for
writing and speaking. In Mrs. Lawrence's first-grade classroom, students use
language frames to compose weekly notes to parents/caregivers regarding their
learning. Over the course of the year, these frames become more complex, as
shown in Figure 4.3.

Gifts of Words

Linking reading instruction with writing instruction is fruitful on many levels. In
the early grades, writing reinforces letter–sound relationships, common spelling

Language Frame Used in Fall	Language Frame Used in Winter	Language Frame Used in Spring
Dear _____, This week in school, we learned about _____. Love, _____	Dear _____, This week in our study of _____, we learned _____. Love, _____	Dear _____, This week in our study of _____, we learned _____. We also learned _____. Love, _____

FIGURE 4.3. Increasingly complex language frames for weekly note about learning.

patterns, and visual cues needed for growth in decoding and word recognition. It also serves to support reading comprehension, since both readers and writers are in the business of making meaning through the manipulation of symbols, concepts, and ideas. In classrooms where students are active readers and writers, opportunities for vocabulary instruction abound. Vocabulary knowledge and control of language are tools writers use to convey very specific meanings to their readers.

In their book *The Word-Conscious Classroom*, Scott, Skobel, and Wells (2008) describe ways to support students in an ongoing process of examining the ways writers write and then appropriating these tools for their own writing. They design learning experiences in which students search for "Gifts of Words" in the texts they read. These Gifts of Words are then collected in word banks, and students are encouraged to "make withdrawals" or to "borrow" from these banks in their own writing. Words can be stored in individual Gifts of Words notebooks, in class notebooks available for browsing, or on index cards. In some classrooms, file boxes keep words on index cards organized by potential use (character words, setting words, action words, etc.). Incorporating a Gifts of Words approach in your classroom increases students' awareness of and decision making about word choice, while simultaneously increasing access to a wide variety of words. It helps students move away from the "happy, sad, glad, mad" phenomenon that many teachers report when describing the words they commonly see in their students' writing.

The Gifts of Words approach is tied to a larger understanding of language and how skillful writers use it. This response to writing is an integral part of the writing process (brainstorming/prewriting, drafting, writing, revising, editing, and publishing), as students respond to their own drafts as well as those of their peers. It is also a way for students to learn about craft, style, and structure from published works by other authors—a technique that has become widely known as "reading like a writer" (Ray, 1999).

As students become aware of the word choices authors make, they begin to discuss possible reasons for these choices. This leads them to consider the idea that text doesn't just mean something to the reader; it can *do* something to or for the reader. It can make a reader laugh, cry, become angry, or make a change. As writers, students begin to understand that they can evoke feelings and emotions, raise questions, or make convincing arguments with the words they use. They can also consider the larger contexts of sentence structure, organization of ideas, and inclusion of illustration or graphics as they affect their creative and informative works.

Think about the Gifts of Words that are *italicized* in Table 4.3, and consider how they might spark discussions about word choice, as well as craft conventions (e.g., simile, metaphor, and alliteration) and their associated academic terms.

TABLE 4.3. Examples of Gifts of Words

Text	Example
Balto and the Great Race (Kimmel, 1999): Third-grade classroom	"In January 1925, winter settled over Alaska like *an iron blanket.*" (p. 9)
The Fighting Ground (Avi, 1984): Fifth-grade classroom	"Softly at first, but with growing sureness, the bell began to ring again. Each stroke *sliced away a piece of calm.*" (p. 5)
Hoops (Burleigh, 1997): Seventh-grade classroom	"The *sideways slip* [of the ball] through *a moment of narrow space.*" (unpaged)
	"Your arm shooting up through *a thicket of arms.*" (unpaged)
	"The *no-sound sound* of the ball as it sinks through nothing but still, pure air." (unpaged)

Word Detectives in Literature Discussion Groups

Literature discussion groups, by their very nature, encourage attention to the words chosen and the language structures used by writers of high-quality pieces. In some classrooms, one task of each group member is to record new and/or interesting words encountered in the reading. In others, each group member is given a particular role each week (e.g., Discussion Director, Connector, Friend of the Characters, Recorder, etc.), with one being Word Detective. The Word Detective's job is to draw the group's attention to interesting and potentially unknown words in the reading, and to discuss ways in which these words reflect the writer's craft and/or ways in which the meaning of the words can be ascertained.

Genre Word Study

In genre word study, students pay attention to and record the types of words encountered in various genres. If they are working on mystery writing, for example, the teacher leads them through a study of the types of words/concepts they've encountered in reading this genre. If they are writing fantasy, they explore the unique features of vocabulary in fantasies, such as the need to make up words to refer to concepts unknown in the real world, and consequently the need to weave definitions of these words into the writing. In addition to books, students are encouraged to consider films representing various genres. Throughout this study, a class chart is constructed showing types of words associated with various genres. Table 4.4 displays words generated by students at various grade levels as they considered various genres.

TABLE 4.4. Genre Word Study Examples

Genre	Grade level	Examples of words generated
Mystery	3	*clue, robbery, stolen, hidden, identity, disguise, detective, crime, police, investigation*
Fantasy	6	*time travel, transformation, incredible, unimaginable, inventions, mad professor, discovery*
Poetry	8	*phrases, metaphor, simile, allegory, alliteration, onomatopoeia, emotion, rhyme*

VOCABULARY INSTRUCTION FOR SPEAKING AND LISTENING

In this section, we turn our attention to oral and aural vocabularies—that is, the words students understand and use in conversation. The speaking and listening strand of ELA is significant in our discussion of vocabulary learning because this strand is not tied to the mechanics of reading and writing. Students who have difficulty decoding words, for example, are not limited in the new words whose meanings they can learn. Furthermore, expressive vocabulary is a strong measure of word learning. When students can accurately and appropriately use a new word in their speaking (and in their writing), they truly know that word. We find it helpful to think about speaking and listening vocabulary in terms of two activities that occur in school: discussion and presentation. Although these activities have been underaddressed in many classrooms, they are highlighted in the CCSS as tied to 21st-century literacy skills. Table 4.5 illustrates the types of words needed for successful listening and speaking. The following instructional approaches support students as they learn the vocabulary of discussion and presentation.

TABLE 4.5. Important Academic Vocabulary for Being Effective Listeners and Speakers

Important word types	Examples	Purposes for which these words are used
Discussion process words	*role, facilitator, manager, recorder, timekeeper, observer, transition, pause, build on, extend, perspective, contradict, agree, disagree, add, question*	To describe ways of talking with others to share ideas and think together.
Presentation words	*articulate, explain, describe, examples, visuals, introduction, conclusion, pacing, eye contact*	To describe the process of reporting information to others, often including the use of demonstration, visuals, or other media.

Buzz Groups

In Mrs. Neal's multiple-age grades 1 and 2 classroom, each day begins with what she calls "Buzz Groups." These are predetermined groups of four, where children congregate as they enter the classroom. From a classroom management perspective, Mrs. Neal has found that it works best to allow students to talk socially before the morning meeting, and Buzz Groups accommodate the fact that students arrive at different times. Once the bell chimes to indicate the start of the school day, Mrs. Neal allows each Buzz Group to share a bit of its conversation with the whole class. The Reporter for the group rotates each day and uses a standard introduction to frame the brief report: "Good morning. My name is Julia, and I am reporting for Trevor, Ethan, Sarah, and myself .. ." Over time, Mrs. Neal teaches her students important words to support sharing information on behalf of a group, such as *summary*, *agree*, *disagree*, *comment*, and *question*.

Guest Speakers and Field Trips

Third-grade teacher Mr. Ryan capitalizes on field trips and guest speakers for teaching academic vocabulary associated with listening and speaking. Before going on a field trip, Mr. Ryan engages his students in study of content related to the field trip, as well as discourse patterns for engagement during the field trip. An excellent way to prepare students for the types of discourse they will hear when listening to a speaker is to show speeches (available online) to the class and to talk through both the content and the discourse patterns in the speeches. In a recent field trip to a recycling facility, he had students fill out a "Know, Want to Know, Learned" (K-W-L; Ogle, 1986) chart after doing research on recycling, so they could identify questions they had not been able to answer but hoped to answer during the field trip. They also watched two brief speeches on recycling, given by students and captured on YouTube. They analyzed these speeches both for content and for discourse elements, noting the persuasive nature of the talk, the use of facts to support major statements, and the use of concrete examples of abstract concepts. By immersing themselves in this type of discourse before hearing talks at the recycling facility, they were prepared for more meaningful listening and engagement with the speakers. Before the field trip, each student wrote three questions on an index card, and practiced asking his or her questions. Mr. Ryan encouraged them to link their questions to their existing knowledge, so that they could engage in more complex language structures representative of academic discourse. Stella came up with the following:

> I have studied the process for recycling glass, and I've learned that it takes 1 million years for glass to break down. A question that remains unanswered

for me is why it takes so long, since glass contains sand and there is a lot of sand on the earth.

Students also have a chance to use these structures when guest speakers visit the class. Mr. Ryan has arranged for small groups of fourth-, fifth-, and sixth-grade students to visit his class each month, in order to share information about their research projects. Mr. Ryan also arranges for local college professors and parents to share information about their work, special talents, or interests. Because of the regularity of these classroom visits, and the expectation and instructional support for academic discourse, Adam's statement to a recent guest speaker (a college professor) is not uncommon:

I have one question and a comment about what Jackson said. My question is "When you work at a college, do you get to sleep there too?" And my comment is "I think it would be hard to deal with older kids when they mouth off."

Procedural Coaching Routine

In Mr. Dawson's second-grade classroom, a procedural coaching routine provides students with authentic reasons for using academic language in order to explain routines and procedures. He selects four or five students each week and teaches them a new classroom routine, such as how to use a new learning center or how to use a new piece of software at the computer station. He then charges each of these "coaches" with the task of teaching the rest of the class. Each coach is responsible for teaching two students at a time throughout the course of the week. The routine is written and placed in the location in which it will be used (e.g., at each computer station, as shown in Figure 4.4). This way, both the coach

• *Sign in*.
• *Log on* with your *password*.
• Find the Reading *folder* on the *desktop*.
• *Double-click* to *open* it.
• Find your *document*. *Double-click*.
• Set the timer for 15 minutes.
• *Save* your document when you are finished.
• *Sign out*.

FIGURE 4.4. Procedural coaching routine: Computer station (academic vocabulary *italicized*).

and those learning the routine have continued access to the routine (and the academic language associated with it) over time.

Class Discussions

We cannot overemphasize the importance of regular discussion for developing the knowledge, dispositions, and competencies related to vocabulary learning and powerful use of language. Class discussions, in which the teacher acts as facilitator and model, but does not dominate as the only source of information, allow students to use academic terms (and embrace the underlying concepts) such as *opinion, perspective, compare, contrast, synthesize*, and *summarize*. A literature discussion group can be a powerful forum for this type of talk because it allows students to attend to the content and use of language in a book, while also attending to the content and use of language in their discussions. Consider the various elements of academic language learning in the following excerpt from a discussion among five eighth graders reading Sharon Draper's *Double Dutch* (2002). Each student has been assigned a role for this discussion, with two students (Tamika and Drew) assigned as Word Hunters because of Draper's use of figurative language and slang. Two students in this group (Anita and Rimma) are ELs.

> LYNETTE (Facilitator): OK, stop talking everybody. For today, we read Chapter 6, and one of the things we're supposed to be looking at is the figures in this chapter. Not the figures .. .what is it called?
>
> TAMIKA (Word Hunter): Figures of speech.
>
> DREW (Word Hunter): Yeah. Ms. O'Bannon also called it figurative language.
>
> LYNETTE: OK, so what did you come up with?
>
> TAMIKA: Well, I thought some of it was figures of speech, like idioms and stuff, and some of it was slang. Like on page 46, Yolanda says, "Don't say 'death'—you're freakin' me out!" "Freakin' me out" is another way of saying "You're scaring me." What do you all think?
>
> RIMMA: I think so. I hear that a lot, "You're freakin' me out; I'm freaked" on TV and with kids.
>
> DREW: Yeah, and in the context it makes sense. Because everyone is afraid of the Tolliver dudes. So I agree. Another similar example I found was on page 52, where it says, "You want to get iced?" The character Aziz says that about halfway down the page.
>
> ANITA: What does that mean? I don't understand that.

DREW: "To get iced" means "to be killed." [Others in the group nod in agreement]

ANITA: [with wide eyes] Killed?! What? Did someone get killed?

LYNETTE: No, they're saying they're afraid that if they say anything mean to the Tolliver brothers, then they *will* be killed. The Tolliver brothers are like bullies in this story.

TAMIKA: Yeah. They go around scaring everybody. So we found two slang words. What about figures of speech?

TAMIKA: "Blow over" on page 54. Yolanda says, "I think this whole thing will blow over." I *think* that is a figure of speech. It's like comparing the Tolliver brothers to a storm that will go away.

DREW: Yeah, I agree with that. Anybody disagree?

BRANDI (Connector): I agree with you. I also saw a connection between this chapter and stuff that goes on in real schools with bullies. I thought the teacher in this story did a good job of talking about fear and intimidation, and how being afraid gives the bullies more power.

DREW: She also was trying to get the kids to look at the situation from both sides—their side and the bullies' perspective. I thought that was cool. 'Cause I'm a big kid, and sometimes kids are afraid of me without even knowing me, just because of my size.

This brief excerpt highlights the role of vocabulary both in comprehension and in conversation. This group's ability to engage in such a focused academic conversation reflects ongoing instruction in conventions of discussion, coupled with ongoing practice. At the beginning of the year, Ms. O'Bannon shared models of effective (what to do) and ineffective (what not to do) literature discussion groups, using video clips and the fishbowl technique. Using the fishbowl technique, she engaged in a model literature discussion with three other adults in the building, while her students observed and took notes. Afterward, the students discussed what they had observed and, as a class, turned these characteristics into a rubric to guide future discussions. Once literature discussions were underway among her students, Ms. O'Bannon adopted the practice of sitting in on two groups during each discussion time period. She recorded her observations, using the rubric to capture the degree to which specific discussion conventions were exhibited by each group. She then shared this feedback with the group members, so that they could adjust and refine their discussions as needed. In cases where groups struggled to adhere to discussion conventions, she appointed one member of the group as observer and rotated this role among group members, so that each member could use the rubric to observe firsthand how the group was working. She found that when students observed their own practice, they could better understand which areas were in need of improvement.

Class Presentations

In addition to participating in discussions, students need to learn the academic vocabulary and discourse styles associated with formal presentations. Common types of presentations in elementary and middle school include presentations to demonstrate understanding related to texts that have been read and/or research that has been done; persuasive presentations, designed to provide information along with a particular perspective on that information; and reflective reports, in which students share their thoughts on a set of information, as in a personal progress portfolio. Of course, presentations are often a mix of these. For example, a fourth grader's report on *Pictures of Hollis Woods* (Giff, 2002) included research on Alzheimer's disease, since this affects one of the main characters in the story; similarly, a seventh grader's report on *The Boy in the Striped Pajamas* (Boyne, 2006) included details about the Holocaust, since this is the central event in this fable.

As in writing a report, when preparing a spoken presentation, students must consider their audience, their purpose, and the main ideas they wish to convey. They must provide enough information to be clear and credible, without providing so much that the listener is lost in a sea of details without an understanding of the key points. They also need to consider whether they will have visuals (or audio) to support what they say, or whether the entire presentation will rest on their words. They must consider the best use of time, so as to keep the audience engaged; and they must consider ways of engaging the audience, including word choice, intonation, and pacing. With respect to visuals, they need to be sure that the visuals complement the spoken portion of the presentation rather than detract from it. They must also work on the size and overall look of the visuals, so that they can be clearly seen, whether in the form of a trifold poster board or a PowerPoint slide show.

Intriguing presentation projects that provide great practice with academic vocabulary are the ones in which students present their academic lives. In one second-grade classroom, this takes the form of a Kid Pix slide show with audio narration, "Life in Mr. Dawson's Second-Grade Classroom," which runs in a loop throughout the spring open house for parents. Older students can put together similar group presentations to share with students in the grade below, as a way of introducing them to the next grade. Or, individually, students can create reflective portfolio presentations of their academic experiences over the course of the year. In Mrs. Rey's sixth-grade classroom, students select a digital tool such as PowerPoint, iMovie, or Prezi to present academic portfolio presentations. In their presentations, they describe and provide examples of major concepts learned in each subject area; the areas in which they have made the most improvement over the year; samples of work they are most proud of, and the rationale for including these samples in the portfolio; and personal academic goals. After they practice these presentations in class and receive feedback from their peers, they refine them for presentation at the final parent–teacher conference of the year, which is attended by parents/caregivers and at least two other content-area teachers, in addition to the ELA teacher.

WORD STUDY: TYPES, RELATIONSHIPS, AND STRUCTURE

hippopotomonstrosesquipedaliophobia (n.): fear of long words

As we've mentioned, word learning is incremental, occurring slowly over time. Therefore, the more information about and the more exposures to new words students receive, the greater their chances for long-term learning and retention of these words. In addition, as students' vocabularies grow, so too does the ease with which new words are acquired. For these two reasons, word study is an important part of a strong ELA program. Word study moves beyond learning the meaning of an individual word to paying attention to a particular feature of the word that also characterizes other words in the language. For example, you may not have known that the very long word above means "fear of long words," but you probably knew that it refers to a fear of some kind. Attending to the composition of the word, coupled with your study of other words containing the root word *phobia*, provided you with a head start in determining the meaning of this word.

Word study includes instruction on relationships among words (e.g., synonyms and antonyms, or words belonging to the same category, such as types of precipitation), figurative language (including idioms and puns, as well as similes and metaphors), and common roots and affixes in our language. By studying word characteristics and composition, students can obtain clues to figuring out the meanings of words that share similar features.

Semantic Relationships

Understanding how words are related to one another is an important component of word learning. In kindergarten, concept books are a fun way to consider opposites (antonyms) such as *up–down*, *inside–outside*, and *over–under*, just to name a few. At this age, Keith Haring's *Big* (1998) is a wonderful way to consider synonyms for *big*, including *gigantic*, *enormous*, and *huge*. After getting to know this book, students can be prompted to think of finer relationships among the words with questions such as these: Do *big* and *enormous* mean exactly the same thing? How are they related? How would you place the following words in order by size: *big, huge, gigantic*? As students progress through the grades, awareness such as this helps to distinguish shades of meaning, as in the difference between *walk* and *meander* or among *run, dart,* and *charge.*

Figurative Language

Figurative language uses comparison, contrast, exaggeration and unusual word combinations to convey meaning. Figures of speech, including metaphors, similes, and idiomatic expressions, convey meanings that are different from the literal interpretation of the words, and often convey more nuanced meaning in this way than would be possible otherwise. Figurative language, which is very common in literature and in speech, can be particularly difficult for ELs and for students whose thinking tends toward the concrete rather than the abstract. Immersion in rich and varied language experiences contributes greatly to students' abilities to begin grasping expressions like these: "He was a stick in the mud" (metaphor), "She ran like the wind" (simile), and "A bird in the hand is worth two in the bush" (idiom). Word study allows for intentional practice with figurative language, as in grades 1, 2, and 3 at Richmond School, where each student adds one entry per week to his or her Idiom Book (see Figure 4.5).

Word Structure

Research points to the benefits of teaching students about the structure of words, so that they can use information about root words, prefixes, suffixes, (including Latin or Greek origins) to determine the meaning of new words they encounter (Baumann et al., 2002; Kieffer & Lesaux, 2007; Rasinski, Padak, Newton, & Newton, 2011). Knowing Latin and Greek roots can be particularly helpful for two reasons. First, they are found in many content words in science, social studies, and mathematics. Second, ELs whose native languages have Latin origins (e.g., Spanish) will find similarities between some of their native words and English words. These similar words are known as *cognates*, and an example is *excelente* (Spanish) and *excellent* (English). Baumann and colleagues (2007) have successfully used prefix and suffix "families" in their work with students in the upper elementary grades. For example, the prefixes *dis-, un-, in-, im-, il-, ir-,* and *non-* belong to the *not* prefix "family" because they all mean *not* or *the opposite of* the word to which they are attached. As these families of prefixes are studied, they can be added to a classroom chart for easy reference. Personal "affixionary"

FIGURE 4.5. An entry for "Raining cats and dogs" in David's Idiom Book.

notebooks (Blachowicz & Fisher, 2010) allow students to record information in personal notebooks. The affixes shown in Figure 4.6 are helpful in determining how best to spend instructional time.

STRATEGY STUDY: USING CLUES WITHIN AND AROUND WORDS

As students learn how to identify roots, prefixes, and suffixes, they can also learn how to use this information as a potential to determine meanings of unknown words encountered both in ELA and in other subject areas. In addition to these "clues within words," students can learn how to use contextual information, or "clues around words," as a tool for independent word learning. Research supports teaching students to examine the context within which words appear for clues to the words' meaning (Baumann et al., 2002). *Context* includes the sentence in

Affix	Meaning	Examples
Prefixes		
co-	with, together	*cooperate, coordinate, coworker*
dis-	not, opposite from	*disagree, dishonest, disappear*
em-, en-	in, to put into	*embed, encourage*
ex-	former, out	*ex-husband, export, excavate*
in-, im-, ir-	not	*inaccurate, imbalance, irregular*
inter-	among, between	*international, intercession*
non-	not	*nonviolent, nonfiction, nontoxic*
over-	too much	*overbearing, overpriced, overeat*
pre-	before	*precaution, prewar*
pro-	favor	*pro-education, pro-environment*
re-	again, back	*replay, redo, revision*
super-	over, more than usual	*superstar, superpower, supernova*
trans-	across	*transatlantic, transport*
un-	not	*unhappy, unfamiliar*
Suffixes		
-al	relating to	*optical, natural*
-ble	inclined to	*sociable, perishable, divisible*
-ence, -ance, -ancy	quality of, state of	*difference, prominence, infancy*
-er, -or	one who does something	*teacher, sculptor*
-ful	full of	*joyful, careful*
-ian	relating to, someone who engages in	*mathematician, musician*
-less	without	*fearless, hopeless*
-ly	in the manner of	*gingerly, figuratively, happily*
-ment	act or process of, result of	*government, fulfillment*
-ness	state or quality of being	*darkness, sadness*
-tion, -sion	state, quality, or act of	*saturation, division*
-ty, -ity	state or quality of	*humidity, honesty, loyalty*

FIGURE 4.6. Alphabetical list of common affixes and their meanings.

which an unknown word appears; the sentences before and after the unknown word; and the larger context of the entire text itself, including the genre (Wieland, 2008). Teaching students to use the strategies of structural and contextual analysis takes time, but it is a worthwhile investment, since these strategies can be used across academic domains and across grades. In the words *invisible, deceitful,* and *remarkable* (in *Invisible Stanley*; Brown, 1996) for example, there are clues within the words. The word *mushers* (in *Balto and the Great Race*; Kimmel, 1999) contains clues inside the word and clues outside the word:

Sled drivers, known as *mushers*, could look at a dog and know in an instant if he was a natural for a team. (p. 5)

It is helpful to guide students in explorations of the types of contextual clues they may find. In this case, Kimmel has provided a definition of *mushers*. Other types of clues include synonyms ("We are a *loquacious* group. We certainly like to talk!"); antonyms ("During classes, the hallways are *deserted*, not filled with kids like they are between classes"); examples ("Huts, cabins, apartments, and houses are types of *dwellings*"); and general clues related to the events, setting, tone, mood, or genre of the text ("The creaky floorboards, dim lighting, and cobwebs gave the house an *eerie* feeling").

Since structural and contextual clues are sometimes misleading, it is always important for students to ask themselves whether the hypothesized meaning, based on the clues, makes sense in the text. One way to reinforce this idea is to have students do a few *vocabulary studies* (Watts & Truscott, 1996), in which they (1) write down an unknown word in text, along with the page number on which it appears; (2) write down any context clues they can locate; (3) write down their hypothesis as to the word's meaning; (4) look up the word in the dictionary, and write down the dictionary definition that makes most sense for the context; and then (5) write a one-sentence statement indicating whether the hypothesis was correct or incorrect and how the clues were helpful or unhelpful. Since vocabulary studies emphasize the *process*, they allow for meaningful teacher feedback and student self-assessment, even when context does not result in an appropriate meaning.

As students build their capacity for using structural and contextual analysis independently, posting and continually drawing students' attention to a vocabulary rule—such as the one adapted by Baumann and his colleagues (2007) from Ruddell's (1999) context–structure–sound–reference strategy—can be helpful:

1. *Context*: Look for clues in sentences around the word.
2. *Word parts*: See if you can break the word into a root and a prefix or suffix.
3. *Context*: Reread the sentences around the word to see whether your hypothesis makes sense.

RESOURCES: DICTIONARIES, GLOSSARIES, AND THESAURI

Providing instruction in the use of dictionaries, glossaries, and thesauri is an important part of an ELA program and will aid students in all content areas. However, students can become rightfully frustrated when they look up a word in the dictionary, only to find a definition filled with more words they do not know! In Chapter 8, we provide a list of recommended resources that are useful for students in grades K–8, with an emphasis on those that are student-friendly. Here we want to emphasize the importance of teaching students to be active and thoughtful in their use of resources, rather than focusing exclusively on the mechanics of accessing resources. Although students certainly need to learn how to use keywords in the dictionary coupled with alphabetization to locate the word they need, they need ongoing practice in interpreting dictionary defi-nitions and determining which of several definitions is the correct definition for their purpose. Therefore, instead of requiring students to copy definitions verbatim, or listing three synonyms for a given word, we suggest activities tied to meaningful use in context. Vocabulary studies, described above, provide a forum for meaningful use of the dictionary in context, and require students to process the dictionary definition located. Other productive activities include using a thesaurus while writing, in order to find a suitable synonym or antonym to convey meaning in a written piece; using a glossary to access a discipline-specific word meaning, and then using that meaning in a thematic concept map or summary of information gleaned from a unit of study; and playing games such as Student Word of the Day. In this game, pairs team up to find a word in the dictionary that is likely to be unknown to others; parse the definition together; and then find a way to teach the word's meaning to the rest of the class by using words, pictures, and/or movement. Other ideas for word games are found in Chapter 8.

USING DYNAMIC ASSESSMENT TO INFORM INSTRUCTION

Powerful instruction is always linked to ongoing and meaningful assessment. This is especially true when it comes to teaching vocabulary because of the incremental, individualistic nature of word learning, which is difficult to capture on standardized assessments. In order to use assessment as a guide for instruc-tional planning, we recommend the following:

- Use knowledge rating charts and student self-assessment to determine which words require instruction prior to reading.
- Collect students' records of their interactions with words, in order to gauge what they are learning about specific words as well as what they are learn-ing about the word-learning process. Items to collect might include lists of words gathered by Word Detectives in literature discussion groups, Gifts of Words, vocabulary studies, and class semantic maps created before, during, and after reading.

- Have students create a word map early in a unit of study, then revisit and flesh out the map midway through and at the end of the unit of study. These work samples provide data on word learning over time and suggest direction for increased word study.
- Play games such as Beck and McKeown's (2002) Thumbs Up/Thumbs Down frequently, and observe students' responses. Students are asked questions such as "If you found $500, would you be *sorrowful*? Put your thumb up if your answer is yes, thumb down if your answer is no." This game can be played as a way of making the transition from one activity to the next or while waiting in line.
- Listen, listen, listen. Observe, observe, observe. Pay careful attention to your students' word choices in conversation and writing, noticing use of words that have been taught. Since word learning is incremental, students will often misuse a new word before using it correctly, and these misuses are cause for celebration (students are trying out new words and working toward making them their own) and rich sources of information. For example, when John recently said, "I feel bad because Nate said I was *stupendous* in the class play," his teacher suspected that he was equating the word *stupendous* with the word *stupid*. She was able to provide on-the-spot instruction to adjust his understanding of this word's meaning.

CONCLUDING THOUGHTS

There are numerous ways to address word learning, both during the ELA block and during other parts of the school day. We recommend integrating learning opportunities into existing classroom routines such as morning meeting, morning message, transition time, handwriting practice, and conversation. New routines, such as Word of the Day or Word of the Week and Word Sightings, can be established for further engagement. There are myriad ways for word learning to be fun, interactive, and a consistent part of students' lives both in and out of school.

DISCUSSION QUESTIONS

1. One characteristic of effective vocabulary instruction is providing multiple opportunities for practice over time. In this chapter, we suggest that making space in the classroom for words as they are being learned encourages this type of practice. Discuss ways you can make space for words in your classroom, so that students are encouraged to recall and use new words after the initial exposure. As you brainstorm ideas, think about how you can draw students' attention to these words on a regular basis.

2. Review the ideas presented in this chapter for teaching the vocabulary associated with reading and writing, such as the vocabulary picture walk, Vocab-o-Grams, vocabulary images, Gifts of Words, and Word Detectives. Discuss one or two that you could most easily integrate into your instruction, including how you can envision this integration.

3. As we have mentioned, listening and speaking are too often overlooked with respect to intentional instruction and practice. Yet they are key components of the CCSS. In what ways can you attend to listening and speaking in your daily work with students? Specifically, how can you support students in bolstering their speaking vocabularies?

CHAPTER 5

Teaching Academic Vocabulary in Social Studies

ANNA: Now, my question is "What do you think is most important in this section I just read to you?"

MARTA: Well, it seems strange that there were so many of these Iroquois people who all lived in the area that is upstate New York. And it is interesting that the name we use, Iroquois, was what the French called them, not their own name. I can't really pronounce that [Haudenosaunee].

ANNA: I think that, yes, I agree with you. It is important, interesting, it is now upstate New York and it is cool if you ever go to the north of New York, you go upstate, you think, like, wow, all the Indians and groups of people were here, they were actually here. Could you tell me more about the Iroquois?

MARTA: The Iroquois are a group of five nations, and those five nations, they were all fighting, but they came together and had peace. They have the Great Law of Peace, and everyone followed that. And basically it said not to kill each other.

ANNA: So what does the Great Law of Peace mean?

MARTA: It means that the Iroquois nations cannot kill each other.

ANNA: That's interesting. I wonder if they still live with the Law of Peace.

This snippet from a discussion between two fifth-grade girls who have learned a partner reading routine—Partner Reading and Content, Too (PRC2; Ogle, 2011; Ogle & Correa-Kovtun, 2010)—introduces some of the issues with vocabulary that social studies presents. It also illustrates how PRC2 provides strong support for students not only in hearing important terms pronounced by their teachers, but also in using those key terms themselves. The PRC2 framework is explained later in this chapter.

As we look back at this short bit of Anna and Marta's discussion and think of the text they are reading, some of the challenges posed by the vocabulary students encounter in social studies texts become clear. First, this text includes several names of key places (*Northeast woodlands, southeast of Lake Ontario, upstate New York*) and Native American groups (*Iroquois, Mohawk, Oneida, Seneca, Onondaga,* and *Cayuga*) that may be unfamiliar to the students. Second, several key concepts, including the ideas of a *League of Nations,* a *confederation,* and the *Great Law of Peace,* are essential. The concept that the early European colonists borrowed ideas for government from the Iroquois League of Nations—a union of five Native American nations that united in a representative government with a written constitution and a commitment to consensus in decision making—means that a great deal of information is associated with the names *Iroquois League of Nations* and *Great Law of Peace.* Not just identifying the terms, but knowing their meanings, is essential. In addition, some basic terms related to Native American peoples, social organizations, and governing need to be understood for the total text to make sense.

Many social studies teachers don't focus instructional planning by thinking of what vocabulary to teach, but they definitely think of teaching and developing students' conceptual understanding. This is just another lens through which to consider academic or domain-specific vocabulary. Much of the content is contained in key terms that students need to internalize. Yet, for students to learn these concepts, it is very useful for them to have a good grounding in understanding how to identify important terms, how to determine their meanings, and how to elaborate and expand on initial understanding as they learn more about the concepts(Ogle, Klemp, & McBride, 2007). Very seldom will the one word with a single definition be very useful in social studies. The meanings of concepts like *representative democracy, consensus,* and *constitutional government* keep expanding as students encounter them again and again—not only in studying the Iroquois League of Nations, but later in learning about the American Revolution and the formation of the U.S. government, and throughout the study of American history and government.

PERSPECTIVE ON DISCIPLINE-BASED VOCABULARY

When we reflect on how to highlight the most important concepts and terms in a social studies unit, there are several ways we can help students learn that are much more effective than simply giving them a list of words to define. We need to help students build associations among terms and create a framework within which new concepts can be related to other knowledge and ideas.

Developing Relationships among Terms

When we want students to make use of the information authors provide, we need to help them become attentive to the key terms being used, to understand those in relation to the concepts being developed, and then to create some associations and links so they can retain those terms in meaning and in pronunciation. In the example about the Iroquois League of Nations, students are more likely to do all these aspects of learning if they mentally create a map of the northeastern United States and associate the five nations with their spatial locations. Connecting the nations' names with their current geographic locations also helps students retain them with visual and associational links. (For example, students can locate lakes, cities, rivers, and falls with names from the Iroquois League of Nations.) In this way, students who are not from upstate New York can build better spatial images of just where this important group of Native Americans lived.

Linking Concepts across Time

Attention to the concepts associated with the governing system the Iroquois developed can also help students understand why these concepts are important. Students can investigate where else the ideas of a League of Nations, representative government, pacifism (in the Great Law of Peace), and consensus in decision making are found or implemented. Linking ideas across time helps students realize that these are important concepts and merit their understanding. Creating a timeline with the beginning of the League as a five-nation group in 1570, and then marking important related events, also can help students understand the length of time being described. (For example, in 1722 the Tuscarora joined the League, for a total of six nations. The colonists borrowed ideas from the Iroquois League of Nations in framing the U.S. government in the 1770s and 1780s.) Time can be a difficult concept for students to grasp, so the visual marking of events on a timeline can both develop familiarity with key concepts and show how they are related.

Connecting to Narratives and Visual Sources

Some students may be more able to grasp the concepts by reading some stories from the Iroquois peoples that underscore the democratic and pacifist values of the Iroquois. Some of these are available online at Native American Facts for Kids (*www.native-languages.org/kids.htm*). Teachers can help students by calling attention to some of the words that are used in the traditional literature, and in the more informative presentations in the other texts they read. Some teachers also help students collect pictures, clip art, or photographs that illustrate important concepts and groups being studied. These concepts might include *longhouses, French settlers, Mohawks, European colonists, forming consensus,* and *woodlands.*

DECISIONS ABOUT WHAT TO TEACH

Every teacher needs to make decisions about what attention to give the development of key terms and how to do so most effectively. We suggest thinking of words in these two key categories (see Chapter 1): *general academic terms* and *domain-specific terms.* Doing so makes it possible to maximize attention to general academic terms that can be used across content-area instruction. For example, students can develop their facility with the academic terms *analyze, illustrate, justify,* and *contrast* not only in social studies, but also as they study science, math, and language arts. It is also important to check to see whether these general terms are used in specific and idiosyncratic ways in social studies, and then to explain these particular uses to students. When social studies texts and assessments ask students to "interpret the past," for example, a specific approach is expected: Students need to use and reference evidence from texts, news articles, primary sources, and other data, not just to share their personal interpretations based on their own experiences. Some of the general academic terms that are often encountered in social studies are listed here:

Analyze	Describe the relationship of . . .
Employ	Apply knowledge of . . .
Explain	Analyze interactions between . . .
Contrast	Use a spatial perspective to . . .
Identify	Understand historical chronology
Chart	Understand and create timelines showing events chunked in periods and eras
Describe	Understand and apply knowledge of historical thinking, chronology, etc., to evaluate how history shapes the present and future
Justify	Use evidence to support a position or idea

These more general academic terms can be developed over time and across disciplines, though teachers must take care to demonstrate variations on how the processes are enacted in each content area.

The majority of the terms students need to learn, however, are domain-specific concepts—for instance, the large numbers of names and locations needed to learn geography, as well as history, economics, and civics. Figure 5.1 shows examples of terms used in some of the specific social studies domains that are developed from primary through upper elementary grades. It is important to be cognizant of which terms are essential to each unit or chunk of content being studied. With this awareness, teachers can make students aware of these terms and help them begin to turn their attention to them. Putting them on the word wall or bulletin board so that they are regularly visible is one good beginning. This lets students know that the teacher considers the words important; students can also turn to the list when they are still unsure of the words they can use, and can take advantage of this quick reminder in their oral discourse or in writing.

Analyzing Word Structures

Another important key in introducing new terms is to help students analyze their similarities and make connections among them. This can occur on two levels: *structural/morphological analysis* and *conceptual connecting*. For example, when students are studying forms of government, they can learn to analyze words like *monarchy*, *democracy*, and *autocracy* and separate the parts that indicate the type of government each is; they can also learn the meaning of *-racy* and analyze the change from *monarch* to *monarchy*.

Figure 5.2 contains illustrations of the affixes and combining forms that are frequently encountered in social studies/history texts. By working together across grade levels, teachers can help students learn to identify and use the meanings of these word parts in building their understanding of important terms.

THINKING ABOUT TEACHING VOCABULARY IN SOCIAL STUDIES

In addition to building some basic orientations to word learning, how can teachers be most effective in helping students develop the academic vocabulary they need to read, write, and engage in academic discourse in social studies content across the grades? As Jeff Zwiers (2008) explains,

> We could spend all day, every day on teaching new content words in research-based ways, but this would take the place of other necessary instruction. Or we could never teach words at all, and let them just sink in—we hope. As usual, we must find the right balance. We achieve this balance when we teach words as tools for understanding and for communicating meaning in our content areas. (p. 188)

Geography	History	Civics	Economics

Primary
Continent
Environment
Prairie
Region
Ocean
Plant cultivation
Desert
	Primary
	Ancient times
	American Revolution
	Christopher Columbus
	Colonial community
	Independence
	George Washington
	Martin Luther King, Jr.
		Primary
		Community
		Cities
		Freedom
		Government
		Mayors and city
		  councils
		Rights and
		  responsibilities
			Primary
			Budget
			Job
			Housing
			Invention
			Resources
			Opportunity cost

Intermediate
Bering land bridge
Earthquake
Far West
Mountain ranges
Continental drift
Climate
Gateway for products
Resources
Mid-Atlantic states
Pacific Northwest
Western Europe
Eastern Hemisphere
Western Hemisphere
	Intermediate
	Abolitionist
	Allied powers
	Amelia Earhart
	Annexation
	BCE (Before Common
	  Era)
	Communism
	Enlightenment
	Colonization
	Great Depression
	Industrial Revolution
	Islamic law
	Immigration
	Native Americans
	United Nations
		Intermediate
		Representative
		  government
		Senate and House of
		  Representatives
		Treaties
		Civil rights
		Constitution
		Patriotic
		Religious freedom
		Statehood
		Tolerance
		Veterans' Day
			Intermediate
			Capitalism
			Tariff
			Tax
			Interest
			Poverty
			Property ownership
			Ruling class
			Workplace
			World economy

Upper
Airborne emission
Aquifer
Arid climate
Barrier island
Biosphere
Biome
Climate region
Drainage basin
Earthquake zone
Fauna
Flat-map projection
Nonrenewable
  resource
Prevailing winds
Weathering
	Upper
	Ancient civilizations
	Arab Spring
	Axis countries
	Egyptian civilization
	Greek civilization
	Hunting and gathering
	Persian
	Andean region
	Assyrian Empire
	Babylonian Empire
	Catherine the Great
	Catholic Reformation
	Crusades
	Neolithic culture
	Renaissance
	Tahrir Square
	Warsaw Pact
		Upper
		Checks and balances
		Constitutional
		  monarchy
		Bill of Rights
		Judicial
		Legislative
		Executive branch
		Civil and criminal court
		  systems
		Election process
		Limited government
		Representative
		  government
		Direct democracy
			Upper
			Agrarian society
			Agribusiness
			Conflict resolution
			Coerced labor
			Demographic shift
			Economic power
			International market
			Labor union
			Market value
			Mass consumer
			  economy
			Protective tariff
			Stock market
			Subsidy
			Unemployment rate
			Wall Street

FIGURE 5.1. Terms used in specific social studies domains.

Prefixes	Roots	Suffixes
a- (not, without)	part (section, component)	-able
im- (not)	port (carry)	-age
ex- (out, from)	agri (field)	-al
de- (out, away)	continent	-ant
inter- (between)	aqua (water)	-ence
anti- (against)	anthro (human)	-hood
arch- (original, chief)	arch (primitive)	-ism
contra- (against)	chron (time)	-ist
dia- (through, across)	crat, cracy (rule)	-ment
ethno- (race, nation)	dem (people)	
mid- (middle)	poli (city)	
pre- (before)	pop (people)	
under- (below)	scribe (write)	
uni- (single, one)	struct (build)	

FIGURE 5.2. Affixes and combining forms found in social studies texts. *Note:* Some suffixes form nouns (*suffrage*), adjectives (*portable*), adverbs (*westward*), or verb forms (*populate*).

We agree with Zwiers that there needs to be a balance between building students' academic vocabularies and teaching the content. Teachers need to pay attention to the terms that are critical to the disciplinary content being learned, as well as attention to the precise uses of language that help students not only learn the content, but also develop general academic vocabulary and an interest in and awareness of the role of key terms. Recent research by Scott and her colleagues (Scott, Flinspach, & Vevea, 2011; Scott, Miller, & Flinspach, 2012) underscores the fact that students need to know a large corpus of words to be successful in social studies learning. With the breadth of content that can be taught, and the frequent lack of agreement on the focus for instruction in the major areas of history, geography, economics, and government, teachers can feel adrift in determining what to teach and to what depth. Given this lack of agreement about many areas of the social studies curriculum, the vocabulary focus needs to evolve from and support the decisions that are made about the content to be taught and learned. When teachers engage in joint planning across several grade levels, more coherence and deeper student learning can be achieved.

It is also clear that students will vary considerably in the depth of vocabulary knowledge that they bring to the study of any particular unit. It is important for teachers to be sensitive to these differences; to help students preassess what they need to learn (e.g., by using a knowledge rating chart, which we have introduced in Chapter 4); and to provide examples of ways students can rehearse and take personal ownership of their vocabulary study. Teachers, rather than assuming that they themselves must determine the full set of vocabulary terms to be learned for each unit, need to provide room for students to create their own collections of new vocabulary terms (e.g., in notebooks used for this purpose). In fact, some studies have shown that when students are given their own choice in what words to focus on, they do as good a job as the teachers in selecting what they need to learn (Fisher, Blachowicz, & Smith, 1991; Haggard, 1982).

THE CCSS AND HISTORY/SOCIAL STUDIES VOCABULARY

This chapter is grounded in the expectation that teachers want to integrate the teaching of social studies content with the language arts processes outlined in the CCSS (NGA & CCSSO, 2010). As has been noted, students need to understand both the general academic terms that are useful for reading, writing, and speaking–listening activities in the classroom, and the content-rich, domain-specific vocabulary. The CCSS also make it clear that students need to develop a deeper knowledge base during elementary school than has been the focus in many elementary curricula: "Building knowledge systematically in English language arts is like giving children various pieces of a puzzle in each grade that, over time, will form one big picture. At a curricular or instructional level, texts—within and across grade levels—need to be selected around topics or themes that systematically develop the knowledge base of students" (p. 33). The CCSS ELA document also provides an example of how teachers can engage in such knowledge building systematically, by planning a clear, spiraling content curriculum around major themes from kindergarten onward: The example shows the topics and areas of the human body systems that can be developed each year, and includes suggested texts that can be used grade by grade to develop this understanding (p. 33). Consistent with this orientation, we also include suggestions for how domain-specific terms can be developed over several years (spiraling from year to year) later in this chapter.

The current emphasis on the CCSS in the United States makes studying these guidelines during instructional planning a high priority for teachers. Therefore, we are including here some of the relevant sections of the *CCSS for English Language Arts and Literacy in History/Social Studies, Science, and Technical Subjects* document.

The CCSS for elementary grades (K–5) embed social studies vocabulary within the general reading standards for informational text. Standard 4 addresses academic vocabulary specifically, with the same expectation for grades 3–5:

4. Determine the meaning of general academic and domain-specific words and phrases in a text relevant to a grade 3 [or 4 or 5] topic or subject area. (p. 14)

In addition, students are expected to develop the "metalanguage" to analyze and study an author's craft and meaning. For example, the grade 5 informational text standards 5 and 8 are shown here:

5. Compare and contrast the overall structure (e.g., chronology, comparison, cause/effect, problem/solution) of events, ideas, concepts, or information in two or more texts.

8. Explain how an author uses reasons and evidence to support particular points in a text, identifying which reasons and evidence support which point(s). (p. 14)

Vocabulary is most specifically addressed in the CCSS language standards 4–6 (vocabulary acquisition and use). The anchor standards state:

4. Determine or clarify the meaning of unknown and multiple-meaning words and phrases by using context clues, analyzing meaningful word parts, and consulting general and specialized reference materials, as appropriate.
5. Demonstrate understanding of figurative language, word relationships, and nuances in word meanings.
6. Acquire and use accurately a range of general academic and domain-specific words and phrases sufficient for reading, writing, speaking, and listening at the college and career readiness level; demonstrate independence in gathering vocabulary knowledge when encountering an unknown term important to comprehension or expression. (p. 29)

These general vocabulary standards are included here because it is clear that helping students develop their vocabularies is a cross-discipline responsibility. It also reminds teachers that students should use the strategies they learn in ELA (including using context clues, analyzing word parts, and consulting reference materials) when they read social studies materials. Too often, students gloss over new and challenging terms without trying to pronounce them or even, in many cases, to develop meaning for them.

The standards for grade 6 and beyond are provided in a special section: "Reading Standards for Literacy in History/Social Studies 6–12." The craft and structure standards for grades 6–8 include the following:

4. Determine the meaning of words and phrases as they are used in a text, including vocabulary specific to domains related to history/social studies.
5. Describe how a text presents information (e.g., sequentially, comparatively, causally).
6. Identify aspects of a text that reveal an author's point of view or purpose (e.g., loaded language, inclusion or avoidance of particular facts). (p. 25)

INSTRUCTIONAL FRAMEWORKS

With the renewed interest in reading history and social studies materials stimulated by the CCSS and the suggestions for creating more integrated instruction, teachers have a good opportunity to rethink their ways of providing both literacy and social studies instruction. We provide two options that have already been developed to strengthen students' learning and command of the academic concepts and vocabulary: PRC2 and the Action Cycle approach.

Partner Reading and Content, Too

We have begun this chapter with a vignette of two girls discussing a text they are reading together. We explain the PRC2 framework in more detail here because we think it provides a structure within which students can take ownership of the domain-specific vocabulary in the units they are studying (Ogle, 2011; Ogle & Correa-Kovtun, 2010). Teachers who use PRC2 first select a set of topical books that are within the varied reading levels of their students. An example of a text set for a unit is provided in Figure 5.3. The teacher matches partners who are reading at about the same level, are compatible, and (as far as can be known) have comparable levels of knowledge of the topic being studied. During any one unit (3–6 weeks), student partners will read at least two of these short texts together,

Text	Reading level
Ancient Egypt: The Realm of Pharaohs, by Cotton, Slice, and Leddy (2001). Publisher: Wright Group/McGraw-Hill.	Grades 4–8
Ancient Egyptian Children, by Tames (2003). Publisher: Heinemann.	Grades 6–8 Fountas and Pinnell (F & P) W–X
Children of Ancient Egypt (*AppleSeeds* Magazine), by Buckley and Butt (1999). Publisher: Cobblestone.	Grades 3–6
Civilizations Past and Present: Egypt, by Supples (2002). Publisher: National Geographic Society.	Grades 3–6 F & P Q–R Lexile level 500
The Great Pyramid, by Thompson (2002). Publisher: National Geographic Society.	Grades 2–4 F & P P–Q
Life in an Ancient Egyptian Town, by Shuter (2005). Publisher: Heinemann.	Grade 4 F & P Q–R
The Great Pyramid of Giza: Measuring Length, Area, Volume, and Angles, by Levy (2006). Publisher: Rosen Publishing Group.	Grades 6–7

FIGURE 5.3. Text set for unit on ancient Egypt.

following a routine the teacher has taught them. They first preview the full text (usually 32 pages) and note the organization and visual components (maps, photos, diagrams, cartoons, etc.). Then they engage in a 2 × 2 × 2 process: The *two* partners start the chapter or section by reading the first *two-page* spread (two adjacent pages) *twice*. The first reading is a silent reading of both pages, followed by each partner's rereading one page to prepare for reading it orally. Each partner also writes a question (usually on a sticky note that can be saved) to ask his or her listening partner. The partner with the left-side page then reads orally to the other partner and asks a good question (one that can't be answered by a yes–no response, but is a "thick, meaty" question). Finally, the partners discuss their responses.

Within 20–30 minutes, the partners can usually read six to eight pages and talk about the content. An important component of this routine is that the partners use the vocabulary and language of the author(s). This ensures that they attend to the language and that they learn to pronounce terms and use good inflection for the presentation of the text. At the conclusion of this reading/discussing phase, students identify two or three vocabulary terms they think they want to remember and write them in their vocabulary notebooks. Some teachers use a graphic guide sheet (see the example in Figure 5.4) that helps students get started with the routine.

Teachers who have used PRC2 as the centerpiece of their social studies instruction have developed a variety of support guides and ways to manage the process. Pre- and postinstruction assessments help them monitor students' growth as the students become more confident in using domain-specific terms and oral discourse (Nagy & Townsend, 2012). See Figure 5.5 for one of the concept-clustering activities used before and after instruction.

---

1. Preview the first two pages you will read together and study photos and other visuals.
2. Both partners read both pages silently, thinking about meaning.
3. Each partner rereads the page he or she is responsible for and writes a question that will prompt discussion of key ideas.
4. Partner 1 reads the page orally. Partner 2 listens and then answers Partner 1's question.
5. Partner 2 reads the next page orally. Partner 1 listens and then answers the question from Partner 2.
6. Repeat this cycle until PRC2 time is finished for the day.
7. Record words that are important to remember in your PRC2 notebook.

FIGURE 5.4. PRC2 guide for reading.

Directions: Choose words from the list below, and put them under the appropriate category or concept. Use as many of the words as you know, and use each only once.

Africa, archeologist, architect, astronomer, decomposing, embalmer, hieroglyphs, pharaoh, preserved, pyramid, quarries, sarcophagus, scribe, tomb, Valley of the Kings

Ancient Egypt

Important Places	Mummification Process	People of Ancient Egypt

FIGURE 5.5. Concept-clustering activity.

Another example of how vocabulary plays an integral part in social studies learning is provided in the following section, written by Robb Gaskins.[1] Before reading this section, you may want to study the diagram he has developed that visually explains his approach to social studies learning (see Figure 5.6 on p. 94).

Teaching Vocabulary in Social Studies (without Even Trying): The Action Cycle Approach

A few years ago, I (Robb) heard Ted Hasselbring speak about developing vocabulary knowledge. At one point, he made a simple statement of an idea I knew well, but on that day, it opened possibilities in my mind I had not fully considered before. He said, "Vocabulary is a label for content knowledge." Although I was well aware that vocabulary knowledge and content knowledge are essentially the same, this statement led me to reflect on the correspondence between effective practices to facilitate vocabulary and content knowledge development. Would I be concurrently promoting my students' vocabulary knowledge if I were using the following practices to deepen their content knowledge?

- Promoting active engagement in a content area by sparking the students' curiosity and encouraging them to generate their own questions and predict the answers to those questions.
- Gently guiding students to make connections within and across topics through the exploration of multiple sources while seeking answers to their questions.
- Providing repeated exposure to central ideas in our curriculum, as well as a rich environment in which students revel in words and discussion as a result of these explorations.
- Allowing students to generate additional questions that promote even greater depth and connections by letting the students pursue their piqued curiosities.

Indeed, these practices seemed to correspond with the guidelines for good instruction found in the literature on both vocabulary *and* content knowledge development. Furthermore, my experience as a social studies teacher seemed to confirm that following these general guidelines would help not only to deepen students' understanding of the central concepts we were studying, but also to strengthen their understanding of the key vocabulary words within and across our units.

---

[1] Robb Gaskins, PhD, is Head of School at The Benchmark School in Media, Pennsylvania.

In what follows, I provide a brief explanation of an instructional approach in which efforts to broaden and deepen students' vocabulary knowledge are completely embedded within a student-generated inquiry approach that encourages discussion as well as repeated exposure to key concepts. This is done through the exploration of multiple sources and the recognition of the cyclical nature of human history. Central to this approach is a conceptual framework I designed called the *Action Cycle* (see Figure 5.6). This framework provides an organizational structure designed to help students understand the causes and consequences of human actions. I start by describing the Action Cycle, and then move on to explain the overarching instructional approach.

In a sense, you can think of the Action Cycle as a story structure for human actions. However, whereas a story structure focuses on providing a framework for understanding *how* the story unfolds, the Action Cycle focuses on providing a framework for understanding (1) *why* the person or group in question has taken the particular action in question, and (2) *what* the implications of that action have been. As such, students can apply this one framework across people, events, and time periods (and across literature and other situations, but that is a different discussion), instead of looking at each new unit or time period in history as an isolated set of ideas, or, at best, a set of ideas loosely connected to the previous one.

The basic premise of the Action Cycle is that humans take actions to meet their most fundamental *human needs* (survival, social, and big-picture needs, as explained below). The way in which they go about meeting those needs depends on the *context* in which they find themselves. Once they take an *action*, those actions have *consequences* that, in turn, change the old context into a new one. This creates a new context within which to take action, and a new cycle begins. To be sure, the actions of other people and outside events also create consequences that can modify a person's or group's context, and this is why these influences appear where they do (in the bottom left corner of the Action Cycle).

Quite a number of key concepts/vocabulary words are built right into the framework and are thereby reinforced on a regular basis. In particular, when students reflect on the *context* in which an action takes place (in their efforts to understand an action or event in history), the framework directs them to analyze the physical and human features of the context. Within each of these categories, the students become extremely familiar with applying important concepts for understanding social studies content. In relation to *physical features*, for example, students are directed to analyze climate, topography, soil, mineral resources, bodies of water, vegetation, and animals. In regard to *human features*, they consistently reflect on population and relevant demographic information, as well as aspects of culture. In reviewing the aspects of culture, the students consider

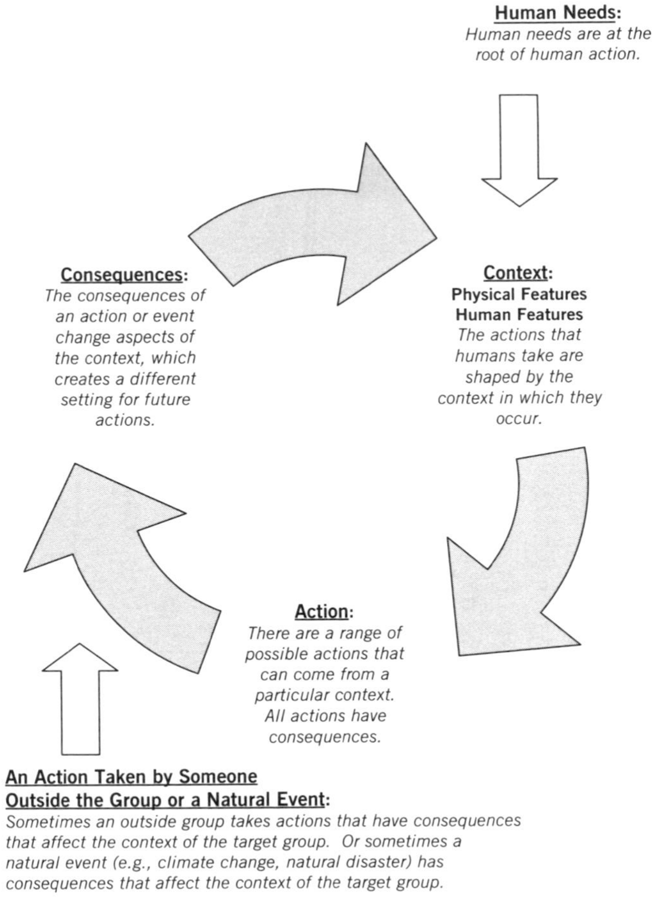

Essential Understandings (EUs):

Human Needs:

EU#1: Humans take actions to meet their needs.
- *Survival Needs:* We need to keep our bodies healthy and safe.
- *Social Needs:* We need to figure out our identities in the group and feel like we belong.
- *Big-Picture Needs:* We need to figure out our identities in the universe and feel like we belong.

Context:

EU#2: The *physical features* of a place affect the actions humans take to meet their needs.
- Use the central physical features as a structure to help find out the physical features that affected the action taken.

EU#3: The *human features* of a place affect the actions humans take to meet their needs.
- Consider the influence of factors related to population and other demographic issues on the action taken.
- Use the aspects of culture as a structure to help find out the human features that affected the actions taken.

Human Needs:
Human needs are at the root of human action.

Context:
Physical Features
Human Features
The actions that humans take are shaped by the context in which they occur.

Action:
There are a range of possible actions that can come from a particular context. All actions have consequences.

Consequences:
The consequences of an action or event change aspects of the context, which creates a different setting for future actions.

An Action Taken by Someone Outside the Group or a Natural Event:
Sometimes an outside group takes actions that have consequences that affect the context of the target group. Or sometimes a natural event (e.g., climate change, natural disaster) has consequences that affect the context of the target group.

Consequences:

EU#4: Human actions (and major natural events) have consequences that can affect the *physical features* of a place.
- Use the central physical features as a structure to help find out the physical features that were affected by the action (or natural event).

EU#5: Human actions (and major natural events) have consequences that can affect the *human features* of a place.
- Consider any changes to the population or other demographic issues.
- Use the aspects of culture as a structure to help find out the human features that were affected by the action (or natural event).

FIGURE 5.6. The Action Cycle. Copyright 2011 by the Benchmark School. Reprinted by permission of Robert W. Gaskins.

the patterns of thoughts and actions a group has developed at a particular time and place that serve as guidelines for taking actions to meet their *survival needs* (related to food, housing, clothing, tools/technology, jobs/economy, health and medicine, and the military), *social needs* (related to communication, leadership/ government, education, sports, and recreation), and *big-picture needs* (related to myths/spiritual beliefs/religion and to scientific studies). Often students consider a consolidated version of these issues. One such example is what I call "The Big Five"—economic structure, technological developments, political structure, social structure, and religious/cosmological structure. Once an action is taken, the students consider the consequences related to the same set of issues.

While the Action Cycle framework is central to this method of facilitating the development of content knowledge/vocabulary, the general instructional approach is essential to obtaining these effects. Each unit follows the same four basic steps:

1. *Generating questions.* The teacher introduces a historical mystery to spark interest, and the students generate questions to investigate.
2. *Making predictions.* The students use their background knowledge, general resources, and the Action Cycle to predict the answers to the central question the group has chosen to pursue.
3. *Developing knowledge.* The students read a variety of texts and review a number of resources in an effort to answer the key question and evaluate the accuracy of their hypotheses, using the Action Cycle as a framework for collecting and organizing information.
4. *Integrating ideas.* The students work together to synthesize the information in a concise and coherent fashion, using the Action Cycle as a framework.

Once the students integrate the ideas related to the current question, the students generate the next logical question (with the teacher's guidance as necessary), and the same pattern is followed until the key ideas in the unit have been addressed.

An example will help demonstrate how the Action Cycle approach facilitates vocabulary development. When I was teaching a middle school class on early civilizations, one of my favorite units to teach was the one on the origins of agriculture. I would begin by building the mystery of why humans switched from hunting and gathering to farming and herding. After acknowledging that the students might not consider this event especially important, I would share that many historians consider this transition to be one of the most important events in the history of the world. Then I would lead them to consider what life must have been like for hunter-gatherers before agriculture. In the next activity, I had them brainstorm how the lives of the group members would have been changed by agriculture.

Once the students were firmly convinced that agriculture was a great innovation, I introduced a quote from Jared Diamond stating his opinion that agriculture was the worst mistake in human history. At this point, I had generated sufficient cognitive dissonance that I could see their mental wheels turning, and they were thoroughly engaged in the mystery. We briefly discussed how agriculture would have made their lives *more* difficult rather than less, at which point I reintroduced the central question: "Why did they do that?" From there, we systematically followed the instructional approach through several cycles of questions related to the origin of agriculture (e.g., "When did agriculture begin? Why did it begin then and not at another time? Where did agriculture begin? Why did it begin there and not in other places at the same time? What were the short-term consequences of developing an agriculture-based society?").

Within the origins-of-agriculture unit, consistent with the guidelines for effective practice promoted in the vocabulary literature, the instructional approach naturally led students to get deeply engaged, make connections, personalize meaning, become immersed in discussion, and receive repeated exposure from various angles to such concepts/vocabulary words as *agriculture, domestication, sedentism, surplus, stable food source, social stratification, job specialization,* and *drought.* Then the students discussed and applied these same concepts and more (e.g., *irrigation, salinization, civilization, complex society, economy, government, organized religion*) as they explored the questions they generated in regard to Mesopotamia. The Mesopotamia unit was followed by a unit on Egypt, in which the students actively discussed and applied all of these accumulated concepts (as well as new ones) as a means of understanding this early complex society and determining how and why it was similar to and different from Mesopotamia. This, in turn, led to the same practice in the next unit, and so on. In conclusion, the Action Cycle approach has proven to be an exciting and enjoyable way to teach vocabulary in social studies (without even trying!).

CONCLUDING THOUGHTS

So much of what our students need to know about the world around them and their place in it is grounded in social studies. Therefore, it is critical that our schools carefully design curriculum and provide powerful guidance and engaging learning activities, so students can understand our history, geography, civic, economic, and political realities. And at the heart of each grade level's expectations is students' development of the concepts/vocabulary that not only will help them learn about the particular topic under study, but will open up connections and relationships across time and space. Students deserve the best instruction we can provide. We hope that this chapter has helped reenergize our readers in their pursuit of this vision and goal.

DISCUSSION QUESTIONS

1. The student dialogue that starts this chapter highlights some challenges posed by social studies texts. How do these reflect your own experience, and what other issues do you find your students facing as they engage in reading informational texts in social studies?

2. We suggest that students become better able to understand academic terms when they develop the habit of looking at the structural components of words. Discuss with a group of teachers what you are already doing to develop this habit and awareness. Also, suggest ways you might strengthen this component of your instruction within and beyond social studies.

3. The CCSS ELA standards include three standards for vocabulary acquisition and use (numbers 4–6) that are included in this chapter (p. 88). How do you assess students' growth in these areas of vocabulary? Which of the areas could use more attention? Discuss with colleagues what you might do together to support students' regular use of vocabulary-learning strategies.

CHAPTER 6

Teaching Academic Vocabulary in Math and Science

Catherine Bernard Petersen is starting a lesson on angles with a fifth-grade special education class.

> CATHERINE: We've learned a lot about angles. Let's review. What is one kind of angle?
>
> STUDENT: Obtuse.
>
> CATHERINE: Take your arms and show me an obtuse angle.
>
> [Catherine models with one arm out parallel to the ground, and one arm halfway between horizontal and vertical. The students do it too. Catherine writes on the board: *An obtuse angle is bigger than 90 degrees.*]
>
> CATHERINE: What is another one?
>
> STUDENT: Acute.
>
> CATHERINE: Show me—with your head as the vertex.
>
> [The students move their arms to show acute angles.]
>
> CATHERINE: An acute angle is a "cute little angle less than 90 degrees." We're missing one.
>
> STUDENT: A right angle.
>
> CATHERINE: Show me—make your head the vertex. It is 90 degrees. It is kind of like an L—it's a perfect L.

The lesson continues with more talk about acute, obtuse, and right or reflex angles. The students use spinners to demonstrate and measure different angles, and to record their measurements.

This math lesson exemplifies some of the differences between the task of teaching vocabulary in math and science (and to some extent social studies), and teaching vocabulary in ELA. In relation to the words themselves:

- Terms have very specific definitions.
- Terms in a given semantic domain may be defined in comparison to other terms in the same domain. Catherine's students understand the difference among acute, obtuse and right or reflex angles because they can see the connections.

In relation to the *teaching* of the words:

- Concepts are repeated several times in any one lesson, and over several lessons, so that students repeatedly hear and use a word in different ways.
- Teaching vocabulary in math and science often involves demonstration and manipulation, especially in primary and elementary grades.

This chapter explores these and other characteristics of math and science vocabulary, examines words appropriate for different grade levels, and suggests teaching strategies.

KEY UNDERSTANDINGS ABOUT MATH AND SCIENCE VOCABULARY

One of the functions of academic language is to describe complexity. Not only is the language in math and science complex (with various grammatical structures), but the vocabulary (and the concepts it represents) is also. Another characteristic of vocabulary in math and science is that words are often learned as part of a semantic network. For instance, a unit of study on weather may include the terms *water vapor, evaporation*, and *condensation*. Such words can be easily linked and may even be defined in relation to each other. A third characteristic is that many words that students come across have more than one meaning; for example, the word *right* in the term *right angle* has no clear connection to a child's right hand. The final dimension we explore is how frequently the words occur in the materials that students typically read and in oral language in the classroom.

Complexity

All content areas contain complex concepts that may be unfamiliar to students. These can be abstract, and may be expressed in phrases (e.g., *solar energy, associative property of addition, line plot*). As content-area teachers, it is our job to teach students about the important concepts in our subject areas. We need to be as efficient as possible in making the complex simple. We know that abstract terms are more difficult to teach than concrete terms (e.g., *photosynthesis* as compared to *stamen*), so we may need to spend more time teaching them. Science includes a great deal of classification, and while teaching the members of a class might be easy, teaching the nature of a class can be more difficult. Finally, although students may think they know the meaning of individual words in a phrase, the combination of those words may be describing a complex concept (e.g., *line plot*).

The density of complex words in a text has an impact on comprehension (Nagy et al., 1987). Consider this example:

> A central concept in semanalysis is the *text*, which however is to be understood broadly as not only verbal or linguistic, but as a trans-linguistic apparatus of productivity. (Semetsky, 2006, p. 25)

What this example demonstrates is that we may disagree on what terms are complex based on our knowledge of the subject matter. To a nonlinguist, the terms *central concept, semanalysis, text, verbal, linguistic, trans-linguistic, apparatus, and productivity* may all seem complex. These are 8 of the 24 words in the sentence—a high degree of concept density. To a linguist, only a few of these words may seem complex. So, as teachers, we need to be aware of which concepts may be complex for our students. We are sometimes so familiar with our subject areas that we can forget how many terms may be unfamiliar to our students. For example, in the sentence "Because of the wide range of organisms, scientists classify organisms so that the study of them can be simplified" (Watkins & Leto, 1994, p. 191), we might focus our instruction on the important terms *organisms* and *classify*. Although these are important, we need to recognize that for many students, the terms *wide range, study of,* and *simplified* may also lead to difficulty in understanding the text.

Science texts often contain multimorphemic words (e.g., *micro* + *organ* + *ism*) in conceptually dense sentences. Such words may pose issues of decoding that need to be addressed even before a student can begin deconstructing the meaning of the sentence. However, such words provide an opportunity to teach and reinforce knowledge of important morphemes.

Mathematics texts may contain long noun phrases with complex grammatical patterning that result in complex meaning relationships. Consider this example:

> You are traveling at 2.4 meters per second. As you travel, your sonar beam moves with you, scanning a rectangular path across the ocean floor. Your sonar beam scans an area of 432 square meters per second. You plan to lower the sonar device so the width of the beam at the ocean floor is reduced by 10%. How much area can your

sonar cover each second with the new beam width? (Willoughby, Bereiter, Hilton, & Rubinstein, 2007, p. 540)

The long noun phrases in this example (*a rectangular path across the ocean floor, an area of 432 square meters per second, the width of the beam at the ocean floor*; etc.), combined with complex grammatical patterning, make the example difficult to understand. However, even complex terms in math and science have *precise* meanings. For example, the *associative property of addition* has only one meaning, although its application can seem complex. In other words, once the meaning of a term has been introduced, the basic meaning remains the same, even when the nature of the concept itself is expanded. For example, a *triangle* is always a three-sided plane figure, even when we add knowledge of particular types of triangles and the properties of triangles, This makes it easier to develop understanding of already familiar concepts as students advance through the grades.

General and Domain-Specific Vocabulary: A Specific Example of Complexity

As we have noted throughout this book, the CCSS (NGA & CCSSO, 2010) make the distinction between domain-specific vocabulary (the concepts in a content area, such as *theme* or *point on a graph*) and general academic vocabulary (words that can be applied across content areas, such as *consist of* or *describe*). Is this a false dichotomy? Some have questioned whether the meaning of supposedly general academic terms is the same across subject areas. In an analysis of the Academic Word List (Coxhead, 2000), Hyland and Tse (2007) found that there was little overlap in meanings across the subject areas for supposedly common core words.

The general meaning of a term may describe different processes in different subjects. For example, although the word *analyze* shares a common meaning across subject areas ("*analyze*: to resolve or separate a whole into its elements or component parts"), the actual applications differ. If we look for examples of the use of the word *analyze* in different areas of the CCSS and the Ohio Revised Science Standards, we can see that the application takes very different forms.

ELA Standards
- Determine central ideas or themes of a text and *analyze* their development . . .
- *Analyze* how and why individuals, events, and ideas develop and interact in the course of a text.
- . . . *Analyze* how specific words choices shape meaning or tone. (p. 35)

Math Standards

- Make sense of problems and persevere in solving them. (*Analyze* givens, constraints, relationships, and goals.)
- Construct viable arguments and critique the reasoning of others. (*Analyze* situations by breaking them into cases, and recognizing and using counterexamples.) (p. 9)

Science Standards

- *Analyze* and interpret data . . .
- Recognize and *analyze* alternative explanations and predictions . . . (p. 3)

What does this mean for instruction? Simply put, teachers will need to teach the meaning of the word *analyze* in the context of how it is being applied. The process of analyzing problems is not the same as analyzing character development. So teaching a meaning of *analyze* may be important in relation to differentiating it from *synthesize*, but teachers will still need to teach a specific meaning in relation to the content to which the process is being applied. This is true not only for *analyze*, but for many words classified as "general academic vocabulary."

The Special Case of Learning Symbols

Students do not just have to learn the meaning of a concept in math and science; they may have to learn two representations of it (e.g., *greater than* and >). Mathematicians will tell you that mathematics has its own universal language, and that this is expressed through symbols. Similarly, many science concepts, such as abbreviations and numbers on the periodic table of elements, are universal.

Learning a symbol is similar to learning a new term for a familiar concept, except that in this case the concept and the symbol may be taught together. If students are already familiar with a concept, then teaching a new term does not require the number of repetitions and examples that are needed if both the concept *and* the term are new. Similarly, teaching a symbol may not require as much practice once the term becomes familiar. In fact, for many symbols (such as =), the icon may become more familiar than the spelled word for that concept.

Semantic Relatedness

As Hiebert and Cervetti (2012, p. 338) put it, "The meaning of one conceptually complex word typically relies on an accurate (and precise) meaning of another complex word."

- Terms are often introduced as part of a unit of study (e.g., *weather conditions, weather patterns*). How they are related is made apparent.
- Terms are often defined in relation to each other (e.g., a *reflex* angle cannot be an *acute, obtuse,* or *right* angle).

In the example lesson taught by Catherine Bernard Petersen and excerpted at the beginning of this chapter, we can see how the semantic relatedness of terms in a math lesson is taught and reinforced. Similarly, in an earth science lesson, the parts of a flower are taught at the same time, and it is inconceivable that a unit on the solar system would not include the names of all the planets and the concepts of *revolution* and *rotation*.

Multiple Meanings

A contrast is often made in vocabulary instruction between teaching a new term for a familiar concept, teaching a new term for a new concept, and teaching a new meaning for a familiar term. The first may be the easiest, and the third the hardest. We know that changing students' misconceptions is harder than teaching new concepts, and learning a new meaning for a familiar term is similar.

A brief examination of the terms in Figure 6.1 indicates how many math terms have a common meaning as well as a domain-specific meaning. Some examples are *set, odd, even, product, mass, plane, compute, decompose, brace, scale, condition,* and *absolute.* A similar examination of Figure 6.2 shows that science terms can also have a common meaning. Some examples include *energy, motion, investigate, atmosphere, force, object, attract, matter, gas, cycle, kettle, elastic, cell,* and *dominant.*

Some research in this area suggests that confronting students with their misconceptions and changing them are necessary. If this process does not occur, students can cling to a misunderstanding that interferes with their learning (Alverman & Hynd, 1989; Marshall, 1989). For example, in one science unit, students' naive conceptions of the concept of *reflection* (in relation to the way light helps us see) included the idea that the sun illuminates an object rather than that light is reflected from objects. Even when they had been *taught* that light is reflected from objects to our eyes, this misconception remained and limited their understanding of the rest of the unit on light (Nussbaum & Novick, 1982). McKeown and Beck (1989) argue that instruction "must consider not only what the students lack, but also the character of the knowledge they already have and the role it may play in representations of new information" (p. 36). An extensive examination of social studies texts (Haas, 1988) revealed that they present a large number of concepts with very little review or reinforcement. Thus students who attempt

Grade	Operations and Algebraic Thinking	Number and Operations in Base 10/Fractions	Measurement and Data	Geometry
K	Set; add; subtract	Numbers to 20; greater than; less than; equal to	Long; weigh; length; weight	Square; triangle; circle; rectangle; hexagon; cube; cone; cylinder; sphere
1	Addition; subtraction; greater than (>); less than (<); equal to (=)	Numbers to 120; place value	Time words	Closed figure; orientation; quadrilateral; trapezoid; half-circle; quarter-circle; half; fourth; quarter
2	Sum; odd; even; equation; array; row; column; multiplication	Numbers to 1,000	Inch; foot; centimeter; meter; minutes; money words; line plot; picture graph; bar graph	Third (of); angles
3	Product; divide; properties; patterns	Interval; equivalent; numerator; denominator	Volume; mass; gram; kilogram; liter; horizontal scale; vertical scale; area; plane figure	Perimeter; polygon; rhombus; parallel; perpendicular
4	Remainder; compute; factor; whole number; prime number; composite number	Algorithm; quotient; decomposition; decimal notation	Formula; ray; intersect; acute; obtuse; right angle	Symmetry; line segment
5	Parenthesis; brace; rule; corresponding terms	Dividend; divisor; scale;	Convert; percent; mean; median; mode	Coordinate; axis; quadrant; attribute; congruent
	Ratios and Proportional Relationships	The Number System (and Statistics and Probability)	Expressions and Equations	Geometry
6	Ratio; unit rate	Greatest common factor; positive number; negative number; absolute value; distribution; histogram; box plot; interquartile range	Exponent; term; coefficient; variable; condition; constraint	Net

(continued)

FIGURE 6.1. Some (not all) vocabulary terms by grade level from the CCSS for mathematics.

Grade	Ratios and Proportional Relationships	The Number System (and Statistics and Probability)	Expressions and Equations	Geometry
7	Constant; proportional relationship; multistep ratio	Additive inverse; integer; random sample; chance; frequency; compound event; tree diagram	Linear expression; rational coefficient	Scale drawing; plane section; supplementary, complementary, and adjacent angles
8	Irrational number; scatter plot; bivariate distribution; slope; intercept; confidence interval	Radicals; square root; cube root; solve an equation	Similar triangle; rotation; reflection; translation; congruent; Pythagorean theorem	

FIGURE 6.1. *(continued)*

Grade	Earth and Space Sciences	Physical Science	Life Science
K	Increase, seasons, temperature, precipitation	Color, size, texture, function, categorize, vibration, pitch	Grow, reproduce, traits, food, water, air, shelter, animal names
1	Energy, exposure, solar energy, solid, liquid	Shapes, heating, mixing, cooling, motion	Investigate, observe, environment
2	Atmosphere, pollutant, mass, speed, vapor, evaporation, condensation	Force, object, magnetic, gravitation, attraction, repulsion	Habitat, ecosystem, fossils, extinct, extant
3	Renewable, nonrenewable, solar panel, electrical circuit, conservation of energy	Matter, mass, properties, gases, liquids, solids, compression	Organism, variation, offspring, genetic, heredity, instinctual and learned behaviors, stimulus, life cycle
4 and 5	Electrical energy, magnetic energy, heat, light, sound, different states, reflection, refraction, absorption, transform, transfer, radiation, convection, conduction	Weight, speed	Environmental changes, detriment, roles of organisms, ecosystem, fossils
6–8	Coal, oil, gas, igneous, metamorphic and sedimentary rocks, tectonic activity, hydrosphere, lithosphere, morain, kettle, esker	Atom, particle, thermal energy, motion of particles, field of influence, mechanical energy, velocity, kinetic and potential energy, energy transfer, friction, elastic	Cell theory, details of reproduction, genetic traits, dominant and recessive genes, codominance, species, mitotic, meiotic, asexual, biome, biotic, abiotic

FIGURE 6.2. Some (not all) vocabulary terms by grade level from the Ohio Revised Science Standards and Model Curriculum.

to merge prior understandings with new meanings in the texts are not given an opportunity to check whether ideas are accurately assimilated before new concepts are introduced.

Research (Marshall, 1989) suggests that students' misconceptions may be addressed in two ways. The first is to modify the texts they read, to directly confront the misconceptions and contrast them with accurate information (Maria & MacGinitie, 1987). The second involves confrontation and contrast in some form of instruction (Marshall, 1989; Nussbaum, 1979). Nussbaum suggests a six-stage procedure, which can be reduced to these three steps:

1. Ask students to explain or demonstrate what they understand about a concept. For example, for the concept *reflection*, ask students to draw a diagram including the sun, a tree, and a boy, to show how light is reflected to enable the boy to see the tree.
2. Examine students' alternatives, asking them to justify their interpretations to each other.
3. Raise questions that encourage students to explore different options (e.g., "When I see my own eyes in a mirror, how does light work?").

For example, a fourth-grade teacher in the Midwest was exploring the concept *winter wheat* with her fourth-grade class. She elicited some conceptions of what it was—wheat that grew in the winter in the plains, wheat grown in the winter in another part of the country, wheat that was planted in the winter. She asked students in groups to explain which of these alternatives was best and why. After a short time, she asked the students whether they knew of any plants that grew in their gardens in the winter, or any plants that were planted in the fall but grew in the spring. Many students mentioned daffodils and tulips. The groups then talked again, referred to the concept in their textbooks, and reported their decisions. Most students arrived at a correct understanding that winter wheat is planted in the fall to allow for an early harvest, but that it does not *grow* in the plains in winter. This type of problem-solving approach encourages students to develop their own understandings when the teacher is not present to help them.

A particular concern involves words that have a different meaning in two content areas. For example, in math one *balances an equation*, whereas in science *balance* is achieved when two *opposing forces* cancel each other out. Also, in this instance, students probably come to school thinking of *balance* as something they do on a wall (or similar). The issue with words such as this, which may be part of a general academic vocabulary, is that it may only make sense to teach the meaning specific to the content area in relation to other concepts in the unit of study. Why would we attempt to teach the mathematical term *balance* in a context other than when we are teaching equations?

Word Frequency

There have been several analyses of words occurring in textbooks (Harmon, Hedrick, & Fox, 2000; Nagy & Anderson, 1984), but two in particular have looked at science and math texts. Butler and colleagues (2004) examined the vocabulary in science, math, and social studies text in fifth grade. As part of a larger analysis, they chose four topics and 12 selections in each subject area, and looked at academic word frequency and type. They limited math texts to word problems, which may have skewed the results, but their study does provide interesting information in relation to a typical text form. Butler and colleagues argue that word problems provide a wider range of language use than other text types in math textbooks, so allow for better comparison with science and social studies text. Table 6.1 provides a brief overview of some of their findings across subject areas. Mathematics had fewer academic words as a proportion of all words in the subject area, where science and social studies were similar. This may have been a function of Butler and colleagues' and Bailey and her colleagues' use of word problems, since other researchers have found that math text contains more academic words than the other subjects (Barton, Heidema, & Jordan, 2002). Interestingly for those who argue we should be teaching general academic vocabulary beyond the specific subject areas, Butler and colleagues found that just 15 out of a possible 275 word types were found in common across these texts. The words included nouns like *population*; the adjective *equal*; measurement words like *pound*; and verbs such as *continue, express*, and *produce*. It should be noted that these numbers do not indicate that in these texts, students would read an academic word every four to six words of text. The majority of most text consists of frequently occurring words—for example, pronouns, conjunctions, and modifiers.

In a more extensive study of fourth- and fifth-grade math and science textbooks that are commonly used in California, Scott and colleagues (2011) have argued that the task of vocabulary learning is even greater than suggested by

TABLE 6.1. Number and Percentage of Academic Words in Fifth-Grade Text by Subject Area

	Math	Science	Social studies
Total unique words	1,964	2,078	3,646
Number of unique general academic words	93 (5%)	224 (11%)	236 (6%)
Number of unique domain-specific academic words	170 (9%)	337 (16%)	639 (18%)

Note. Data from Bailey et al. (2004) and Butler et al. (2004).

Butler and her colleagues. Whereas the latter used sample passages from texts, Scott and her colleagues used complete textbooks—two at each grade level. They asked teachers to identify words that they thought would be unfamiliar or conceptually new to students in these grades. Table 6.2 includes some of their results.

Scott and colleagues (2011) found 987 discrete word families in math and 499 in science. Although they did not report the total number of unique words from which these families were drawn, they give a startling landscape of the tasks that face our students. How do we account for the different findings in these studies? First, Butler and her colleagues used samples rather than complete texts. Second, Scott and her colleagues asked teachers to identify the new concepts, whereas Butler and her colleagues used academic word lists to identify the words. Scott and colleagues compared their word corpus to the Academic Word List (Coxhead, 2000) and found just 13% of the words represented. This raises issues of whether Coxhead's list or Scott and colleagues' is the better source of academic words. Third, the Butler and colleagues study only looked at fifth-grade texts, whereas Scott and colleagues looked at two grade levels. Fourth, the manners of identifying word families and word types may have been different in the two studies. What is of consequence is that both identified a large number of academic words that needed to be learned in math and science in the upper elementary grades. The implications of these findings are addressed later.

Hiebert and Cervetti (2012), in their exploration of the frequency of words in science text in comparison to ELA text, have categorized words as being high-frequency, moderate-frequency, or rare. They base this categorization on the British National Corpus (*www.natcorp.ox.ac.uk/corpus*), which includes approximately a million words, of which 80% were drawn from written texts. The most frequent words are not just function words, but are often polysemous words, such as *object* and *matter*. Clearly such words can cause confusion for students when they occur in science texts (for example), where they have specific and not common meanings. About 5,000 words appear in English with moderate frequency (10–99 times per million words). This means that repeated exposure in narrative texts will provide opportunities for students to learn the words. The

TABLE 6.2. Conceptually New Words in Fourth- and Fifth-Grade Math and Science Texts

	Math	Science	Total	Overlap
New words	4,035	2,838	6,883	
Discrete word families	987	499	1,247	239 (19%)

Note. Data from Scott, Flinspach, and Vevea (2011).

remaining words occur rarely (1–8 times per million words). Some of these may be synonyms for known concepts (*shimmering*), but many will not. However, they may belong to a morphological family, which could result in a frequency of the morpheme five or six times that of an individual word in the family (Nagy & Anderson, 1984). Hiebert and Cervetti argue that rare words are those most likely to be unfamiliar to students and may need to be taught. They compared a text from ELA to one from science, and found that twice as many unique words in the ELA text as in the science text fell into the rare category. However, few of the rare words appeared more than once in the ELA text, whereas individual rare words appeared an average of five times in the science text.

Analyses of the frequency of words in text are helpful, but perhaps more so in relation to ELA. In science and social studies, students may experience many "rare" words in oral language, both speaking and listening. We explore this further in our discussion of instruction below. In addition, although teachers in all subject areas may advocate and try to implement a "spiraling" curriculum, in math and science it is more obviously applied. We understand that word learning is a process of knowledge accretion, and that learning and using a concept in later grades will depend on a full understanding of a less complex concept in earlier grades. Figure 6.3 provides examples of a spiral curriculum as it relates to specific areas of math and science.

Many of us as teachers have either thought or said with incredulity, "What did your previous teacher teach you?" We generally find that students *do* have an understanding of the concepts we are exploring, and that our job is to elaborate and develop that understanding. Figure 6.3 shows how a later understanding of right rectangular prisms depends on an earlier understanding of two-dimensional figures, which is dependent on learning in the primary grades about different shapes and their attributes. Similarly, in the earth sciences, understanding gravitational energy change is dependent on knowing about various forms of energy, which is dependent on learning in the primary grades about weather and energy change. Although this may seem obvious, given that the CCSS were developed in this manner (i.e., downward spiraling), perhaps the implications for vocabulary instruction are not always fully understood in terms of how frequently words are experienced.

We are not suggesting that the idea of a spiral curriculum does not apply to language arts and social studies; it clearly does. As outlined in previous chapters, concepts are learned and developed as students go up the grades. The difference lies, perhaps, in the specificity of the concepts in science and mathematics. For instance, an *acute angle* can only mean one thing, whereas concepts such as *theme* or *democracy* are less easily taught because they have so many different iterations.

	Geometry		Earth and Space Sciences	
Grades	Standards	Example Vocabulary	Topic	Example Vocabulary
K–2	Identify and reason with shapes and their attributes.	*Triangle, quadrilateral, hexagon, polygon, cube*	Weather is a result of energy change. Heating and cooling of water, air, and land (from sunlight) are directly related to wind, evaporation, condensation, freezing, thawing, and precipitation.	*Condensation, evaporation, density, convection*
3–5	Draw and identify lines and angles; classify shapes by properties of lines and angles; and graph points on the coordinate plane to solve real-world and mathematical problems.	*Line segment, parallel lines, acute angle, right angle, obtuse angle, axes, coordinates, hierarchy of two-dimensional figures*	Changes in energy and changing states of matter are explored in greater depth through applications other than weather. Renewable resources (energy sources) and changes in Earth's environment through time are examined.	*Electrical energy, magnetic energy, erosion, matter*
6–8	Solve problems involving area and volume. Draw, construct, and describe geometrical figures.	*Right rectangular prisms, parallel lines, rotations, reflections*	Changes of state are explained by molecules in motion, kinetic energy, and potential energy. The hydrologic cycle and thermal energy transfers between the hydrosphere and atmosphere are studied.	*Particles, conservation of energy, gravitational potential energy*

FIGURE 6.3. Examples of spiral curriculum in math and science.

KEY UNDERSTANDINGS ABOUT VOCABULARY INSTRUCTION IN MATH AND SCIENCE

Given that the nature of the vocabulary to be learned is often more specific in math and science than in ELA, there are some characteristics of instruction that differ from those in ELA classrooms. In the latter, teachers are often concerned about which words to teach, and various ways of choosing appropriate words have been proposed. In math and science, the domain-specific vocabulary to be taught is usually specified in the curriculum. There is less variation in what is taught across classrooms, and specific meanings are often provided in textbooks and curriculum guides. To the extent that word choice is less of an issue, a teacher's task in relation to word learning is that much easier. However, there is a caveat to this: The small words, especially in word problems, are often the ones that can cause difficulties. For example, *compare*, *design*, *look*, *work*, *average*, *equivalent*, *vary*, and *reasonable* are all words with common meanings that may have explicit meanings in math.

The way that important concepts are introduced may also differ across the subject areas. Bailey and colleagues (2004) looked at the academic language used by teachers and students in fourth- and fifth-grade science classrooms. They found that teachers did the following:

- Often gave informal rather than explicit definitions of new domain-specific terms.
- Used explanation (and, less frequently, description and comparison) to introduce new academic vocabulary.
- Often asked students questions about the meaning of academic terms as a review, with frequent reference to their science notebooks or textbook glossaries.
- Used visual synonyms, in addition to verbal synonyms, to support vocabulary learning.

They summarized their findings as follows:

> A range of nonspecialized and specialized academic vocabulary was observed during science lessons. . . . Overt instruction of specialized vocabulary occurred more often than nonspecialized vocabulary, and frequently took the form of examples in the process of providing description, explanation, and comparison of science concepts. (Bailey et al., 2004, p. 86)

In these particular classrooms, the authors observed less overt instruction of academic vocabulary than they expected. However, when it was observed, teachers used various ways to familiarize the students with the concepts. One concern with research such as this, where teachers are observed for a limited time (in this instance, for two sessions), is that the repetition that is common in science classrooms may be missed. That is, a term may be introduced, and then the definition may be elaborated over an extended period.

The Importance of Repetition and Review

We know that a word must be experienced repeatedly in different contexts to be learned (see Chapter 3). The word should be repeated both in one particular lesson and across lessons. Even though the following example comes from only one class period, you can see how important terms are repeatedly used by the teacher and the students in the course of the lesson. The characteristics of insects have been introduced in a previous lesson, so the focus of this lesson is on drawing a contrast between insects and spiders.

Katie Brown is teaching a science lesson about spiders to second-grade students. The text is *Science Horizons, Grade 2* (Silver Burdett & Ginn, 1991).

> KATIE: [Writes on a chart board.] Who can name the animal groups we have learned so far?
>
> STUDENTS: [Offer the terms *mammals, reptiles, fish, birds, amphibians, insects*.]
>
> KATIE: What does it mean to classify animals?
>
> STUDENTS: Put in groups.
>
> KATIE: Who can tell me about insects? Turn to your neighbor and tell all you know.
>
> STUDENTS: [Share what they know with each other.]
>
> KATIE: Now tell me all you know. [She accepts students' terms and draws a concept map (Figure 6.4) on the chart board. She then reviews the three body parts by having them touch their own bodies.]
>
> KATIE: They have an *exoskeleton*—that is, a hard outer shell. Open your book to page 32 and look at the pictures of spiders. OK, let's read a little about spiders. Then I have a video, and then we will compare spiders and insects. [She reads the text, and students follow.] Now turn to your neighbor and tell two things you have learned about spiders.

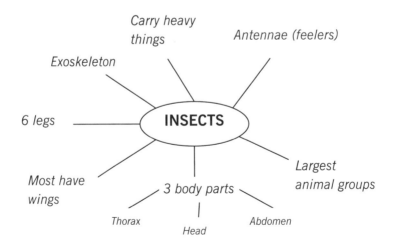

FIGURE 6.4. A map for insects.

STUDENTS: [Share what they have learned with each other.]

KATIE: OK, what is it that we just read about spiders? [She accepts students' contributions and puts them in a concept map (Figure 6.5) on the chart board.]

KATIE: Let's keep reading page 53. [Reads aloud.] Are insects *cold-blooded* or *warm-blooded*? What does that mean? Their temperature changes according to where they are. [She then introduces more new terms and reviews others on the board: *arachnid* for spiders; *exoskeleton; thorax; abdomen.* She asks the students to repeat each word.]

[The students next watch a *Wild by Nature* video about the difference between arachnids and insects, which raises the same concepts as those in the insects concept map (Figure 6.4). After this, Katie introduces a new activity by handing out some sheets of paper and spinners.]

KATIE: Cut out the spider wheel. [There are four concepts on the wheel: *spin silk, 8 legs, 2 body parts, 6–8 eyes.*] Turn your spinner to where it says *6–8 eyes.* Turn to the right. What's the next one?

STUDENT: [reading] They can spin silk.

KATIE: Turn it again.

STUDENT: [reading] They have eight legs.

KATIE: How is that different from insects?

STUDENT: They have six legs.

KATIE: Turn it again. [This sequence continues through the remaining two concepts on the wheel.] I am going to give you pictures of some bugs, and you have to sort them into insects or spiders. [The pictures include a ladybug, a grasshopper, a fly, an ant, a mosquito, and five spiders.]

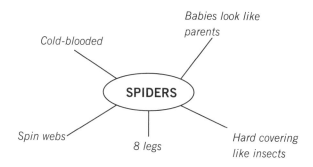

FIGURE 6.5. A map for spiders.

[The students work in pairs to put the pictures in two piles at their tables. Katie uses a stick board with two columns labeled *insects* and *spiders*. Students come up and put their pictures in the appropriate column.]

KATIE: Let's look at the board. Here are some labels. Let's see if we can put them in the correct place on our Venn diagram [Figure 6.6]. Who can use a sentence that tells about both spiders and insects? I'll do one first. [She demonstrates with *cold-blooded*.]

STUDENT: [Makes a sentence with *exoskeleton*.]

KATIE: Who can use a sentence that compares the two? For example, spiders spin webs, but insects do not.

STUDENTS: [Complete more sentences.]

This lesson demonstrates how:

• Concepts (such as *exoskeleton*) are introduced and reviewed over an extended period.
• A teacher and students continually review terms during a lesson.
• A teacher reinforces concepts (such as *thorax*) through manipulation and by using physical examples.
• Different media (graphics, pictures, videos, print) can be used to reinforce concepts.

If we look back to the excerpt from Catherine Bernard Petersen's lesson about angles at the beginning of this chapter, we can see some of the same characteristics

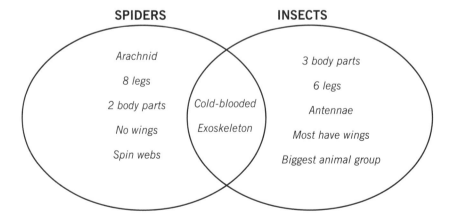

FIGURE 6.6. Venn diagram for insects and spiders.

of instruction. In math in particular, students' knowledge of concepts builds across the grades.

The Importance of Manipulation

We have touched on the importance of manipulating objects as a way of exploring concepts in relation to Catherine Bernard Petersen's and Katie Brown's lessons. However, the manipulation of objects is not enough by itself; there must also be talk about the manipulation that includes use of the important concepts.

In the next example lesson (adapted from an eighth-grade lesson by Wendy Mohrenweiser and Liz Gates), students were asked to decide which of two cylinders had the greater volume. They reviewed some important terms, such as *diameter, circumference, radius, pi,* and *area of a circle,* and discussed the relations among them. They then worked in groups, using rulers, tape, and calculators, to complete the problem sheet shown in Figure 6.7. Every person in the group had to write the same information and agree with it. In the left column, each step in the problem solution was written in words; in the right column, the math calculations were written in symbols. The students then shared their solutions with the class, using a projector. During this lesson, the important concepts were experienced repeatedly: They were heard, read, spoken, seen, written, manipulated, related to each other, and represented by symbols. In addition,

- The terms were applied in meaningful ways to solve a problem.
- Knowledge of the terms was built on previous understandings.
- Knowledge of the terms was extended.
- New knowledge was related to previous learning.

The linking of manipulation with use of the language is important in such learning experiences.

The Importance of Visual Representation

Another common thread in math and science is the interpretation of graphs and charts. Many students start learning about graphs in kindergarten with a bar graph. Learning the specific vocabulary related to graphs comes later, and this vocabulary is expanded across the grade levels. In both math and science, students learn how to construct graphs and charts, and this is related to their interpretation. In other words, students learn by doing.

Talking about science charts can begin early. For example, Blachowicz and Obrochta (2005) suggest a strategy they call *Vocabulary Visits,* which uses the characteristics of good field trips as principles for introducing science concepts/

Problem: Using two sheets of 8½-inch by 11-inch paper, construct two cylinders by sticking opposite edges together—one cylinder with a height of 11 inches, and one with a height of 8½ inches. Which cylinder will have the greater volume? Or will the volume be the same?

Prediction: _____

Use the chart below to describe the steps your group used to solve the problem.

Step	Words	Math Symbols
1	First we measured the diameter of the base of each cylinder.	D1 = D2 =
2	We then calculated the radius by dividing by 2.	R1 = R2 =
3		
4		
5		
6		
7		

Use the back of the paper for more steps. Be ready to share your solution with the rest of the class.

FIGURE 6.7. Problem sheet.

vocabulary and making topical word walls for each unit. The principles of effective field trips, which serve as the basis for this strategy, include the following:

- Good field trips have a content focus. They connect to the curriculum and its content, which provide an integrated context for learning and a relational set of concepts and terms.
- Good field trips are preceded by activating background to "plow the soil" for planting the seeds of new learning. Students know what they are going to encounter, and often teachers do a read-aloud to get them ready.

- Good field trips involve the mediation of an adult. A docent, teacher, parent, or other chaperone is there to help explain, clarify, focus, or point out interesting things, and to question and clarify meanings.
- Good field trips engage students in exploration, talk, reading, and writing.
- And they involve follow-up of new concepts and terms.

An important component of Vocabulary Visits is the use of semantic charting and sorting. Students first engage in brainstorming and chart their personal ideas related to the topic.

For example, prior to a unit on sound, one third-grade EL student's personal chart contained only four words: *noise, loud, shout, music*. The teacher then read aloud an orienting book, *ZOUNDS!: The Kids' Guide to Sound Making* (Newman, 1983), asking students to listen for words they thought were important. Then the students began a group unit word wall, which they elaborated and added to as their study of sound proceeded (see Figure 6.8). Because this was a two-way immersion class, words were added in both Spanish and English, as students noted which terms they encountered in their reading that were important. They were guided to use boldface type and frequency to select important words that everyone should know. As students added their selections of important words, a dynamic unit chart was built.

Throughout the unit, the teacher consistently asked students to participate in semantic sorting and charting activities. For example, students were asked to organize into two columns the following words: *volume, high, low, rich, loud, frequency, pitch, intensity, weak*, and *soft* (see Figure 6.9). Working as teams and

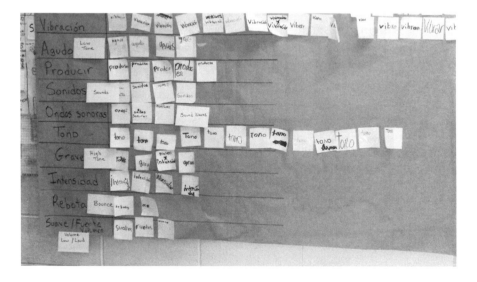

FIGURE 6.8. Class word chart: Spanish and English.

Essential Characteristics of Sound	Descriptive/Related Words for Sounds
Volume	Loud or soft intensity
Tone = quality of sound	Rich or weak
Pitch	High or low frequency

FIGURE 6.9. Two-column word sort.

then jigsawing their team products, they completed this class sort. Other activities included making semantic maps, designing matching games, and writing lab reports.

At the end of the unit, student teams used Wordle (*www.wordle.net*) to construct "word clouds" as a final assessment. The word cloud in Figure 6.10 was completed by the same student who had four words in his relational vocabulary on sound at the beginning of the unit. The word clouds were kept in students' vocabulary notebooks, and the class chart was rolled up and placed in a bin for students to consult whenever they needed sound words for their reading, writing, or other expressive activities.

Word Problems

Word problems in math are universal; they ask students to engage in particular kinds of thinking in relation to a text. Here are some difficulties that students commonly experience with word problems:

1. The supposedly small words in word problems (e.g., *compare, design, look, work, average, equivalent, vary*) can be an issue.
2. The placement of the main idea in word problems differs from its placement in other texts.

FIGURE 6.10. Student word cloud.

3. The syntax of word problems may be unfamiliar.
4. Students may have problems deciding which details are important.

Various ways of teaching students a process for solving word problems have been suggested, such as teaching important phrases and expressions (Zwiers, 2008). Two approaches of particular interest are described by Fogelberg and colleagues (2008) and Hyde (2006).

Fogelberg and her colleagues (2008) recommend a bookmark that helps students think of strategies they can use to solve word problems. The bookmark includes *reading, thinking, paraphrasing, visualizing, representing, solving*, and *explaining/justifying*—each with a drawing as a reminder. Reading and thinking are self-explanatory. Paraphrasing asks students to retell the problem in their own words. Visualizing means drawing components of the problem. For example, if the word problem is about a bicycle and how far it goes in a certain time, the drawing might involve placing a bicycle on a timeline. Representing may include drawing, but also diagramming the problem—for example, drawing the number of coins that are involved in the problem. Solving is the result of the process, and the explaining/justifying step occurs when the students describe their results and reasoning to each other. The following is a typical fourth-grade word problem:

For your birthday, your grandparents give you $50. You want to spend all the money and have none left. You can spend it on movie passes ($12 each),

FIGURE 6.11. A word problem diagram.

DVDs ($14 each), or a ticket to the circus ($22). Which combinations will allow you to spend all the money?

A student might use the diagram in Figure 6.11 to come up with a solution.

Hyde (2006) suggests an adaptation of K-W-L (Ogle, 1986) as a way of helping students solve math problems. K-W-C stands for "What do I Know for sure? What do I Want to find out? Are there special Conditions I have to watch out for?" Using this method for solving the same word problem, a student might complete the worksheet in the way shown in Figure 6.12. Clearly these methods have similarities, which include ways of breaking the problem into understandable parts (although these ways differ), and then representing the process in some manner. Either method will require considerable teacher modeling and practice.

Teaching Morphemes

As a result of their work, Scott and her colleagues (2011) argue that academic vocabulary instruction in math and science benefits from a generative approach that includes the teaching of morphemes. A *morpheme* is the smallest unit of meaning in a language. For example, *cats* has two morphemes: *cat* and the plural *-s*. There are several common morphemes in math and science, some of which can be seen in Figures 6.13 and 6.14. Many math and science words consist of two morphemes—for example, *biology* or *omnivore*.

Two basic processes may be appropriate for helping students develop morphological awareness: *decomposition* of words into their morphemes, and the *derivation* of complex words. In the first process, the students look at a word

What do you Know for sure?	What do you Want to find out?	Are there any special Conditions?
Movies = $12 DVDs = $14 Circus = $22	How many ways can you make $50?	Spend ALL the money.

Show how you solved the problem. You can use pictures, numbers, and words.

I can buy 1 ($12), 2 ($24), or 3 ($36) movie passes.
I can buy 1 ($14) or 2 ($28) DVDs.
I can buy 1 ($22) circus.

2 DVDs = $28 + circus ($22) = $50
3 movies = $36 + 1 DVD ($14) = $50

FIGURE 6.12. A K-W-C worksheet.

Morpheme	Meaning	Math Usage
Ampl	Large, wide	Amplitude, amplification
Centri, cenetri	Center	Concentric, centripetal
Con	With, together	Converge, convert, conjoin
Equi	Equal	Equidistant, equilibrium
Form	Shape	Formula, uniform
Fract, frag	Break	Fraction, fragment
Graph	Written	Graph, graphic
Magn, maj	Great	Magnitude, major, magnify
Medi	Half, middle, between	Media, medium
Meter	Measure	Meter, thermometer
Multi	Many	Multiply, multiple
Numer	Number	Numeral, numerator
Poly	Many	Polyhedron, polygon
Rad	Ray	Radius, radial
Sphere	Ball, sphere	Hemisphere
Number		
Bi	Two	Bilateral
Tri	Three	Triangle, trisect
Quad	Four	Quadrangle, quadrant
Hex	Six	Hexagon, hexachord
Deca	Ten	Decimal, decathlon
Kilo	Thousand	Kilometer

FIGURE 6.13. Common math morphemes.

and decompose it to find the root word that would be appropriate in a phrase or sentence. The phrase or sentence scaffolds the task by providing meaning. For example, students could be asked to decompose the word *microscopic* in the heading "The Microscopic World of Viruses" in a science text. An additional part of the exercise could be to ask the students to indicate the morphemes by marking them in some way (drawing a box around it or using a highlighter). Decomposition is best taught by using several members of a word family: for instance, *photograph, photosynthesis, telephoto,* and *photogenic.* The second basic process is derivation—putting morphemes together. This is harder and is best practiced with words that are already familiar to students. They might be supplied with a list of morphemes that are prefixes and a list of roots; they might then be asked to

Morpheme	Meaning	Science Usage
Astro	Star	Astronomy, astronaut
Bio	Life	Biology, biome, biosphere
Chlor	Green	Chlorophyll, chloroplast
Eco	Habitat	Ecology, ecosystem
Hydro	Water	Hydrogen, hydroelectric
Meta	Change	Metamorphosis, metabolism
Micro	Small	Microscope, microorganism
Logy	Science	Biology, geology, physiology
Photo	Light	Photosynthesis, phosphorescent
Sym, syn	Together	Symmetry, symbiosis
Therm	Heat	Thermal, thermometer
Vor	Eat	Omnivore, carnivore, herbivore

FIGURE 6.14. Common science morphemes.

combine them into words with which they are familiar, and to use those words in a sentence. When morphemes are taught, it is important for students to engage in the repetition and practice that are essential for all word learning.

Another form of morpheme instruction is helpful in teaching ELs. Scott and colleagues (2011) found that 68% of the words in their word corpus, and 71% of the science words, were Spanish–English cognates. Bravo, Hiebert, and Pearson (2007), in their analysis of science texts, also conclude that a significant portion of science vocabulary does relate to high-frequency Spanish words, and that this should be used to enhance the learning of bilingual Spanish-speaking students.

CONCLUDING THOUGHTS

Math and science instruction in grades K–8 is complex. But it can also be exciting and engaging. Teaching academic vocabulary in these content areas is generally thought to consist primarily of teaching the major concepts that are part of the disciplines. What we have suggested in this chapter is that it is that, but it is more than that. There is so much academic vocabulary in these areas that it is important for us to immerse our students in a world of words, use them, write them, and have them speak and write them. It is exciting to introduce students to new ideas and new concepts, so we need to model this enthusiasm as part of our instruction.

DISCUSSION QUESTIONS

1. How often do you use the term *analyze* in your classroom? List some examples, and then think about how the term's meaning might differ in these examples.

2. Brainstorm some vocabulary terms that you use in one of your math or science units. Organize them into a semantic map (or some other graphic organizer) to show the relationships among these terms.

3. What are some of the common difficulties that your students experience with math word problems? How do you currently address these? Which of the suggestions in this chapter do you think might work for you and your students?

CHAPTER 7

The Role of Technology in Learning Academic Vocabulary

Becoming literate within and across disciplines involves learning the ways that experts work with texts within and across disciplines and, in turn, developing a fuller understanding of how knowledge is produced in the disciplines. . . . In the 21st century, this endeavor increasingly involves working with/in networked information and communication technologies (ICT), especially the Internet with its varied text formats and structures such as interactive texts, nonlinear hypertext, and multimedia texts.

—DAMICO AND BAILDON (2011, p. 234)

KEY UNDERSTANDINGS ABOUT ACADEMIC VOCABULARY AND TECHNOLOGY

Recent research suggests that the average student between the ages of 8 and 18 spends over 7 hours a day participating in various technologies (Rideout, Foehr, & Roberts, 2010). Even young children are regularly engaged with technology, according to Vandewater and colleagues (2007), who studied children under the age of 6, and Dodge, Husain, and Duke (2011), who studied 37 children in kindergarten through grade 2. Dodge and colleagues found that 84% of their sample reported using the Internet outside of school. Prensky (2001) refers to students growing up today as "digital natives," a term that highlights their frequent and natural interactions with digital technologies. When used wisely, new technologies offer a range of opportunities to enhance students' learning across the curriculum, and this includes strengthening their academic vocabulary knowledge. In fact, many features of new technologies correspond well with characteristics of effective academic vocabulary instruction.

New technologies allow multiple types of information about a word (e.g., definitions in various styles coupled with varied contexts for the word) to be presented in multiple formats (e.g., diagrams, photos, videos, demonstrations, songs). In addition, the interactive nature of new technologies allows students to manipulate new words and concepts, make connections between and among new concepts, and connect new concepts to existing knowledge. Thus new technologies are engaging not only in the affective sense, but also in the cognitive sense. They allow for active cognitive processing of new concepts.

Mrs. Corbin, a fifth-grade teacher, believes that the Internet offers invaluable resources for learning vocabulary in science. She says:

> What I find so helpful is that there are so many different ways to access information about a word, and with so many different kinds of learners in the classroom, having multiple options is fantastic. Just recently we were studying photosynthesis, and this is always a complex concept for my students, with a lot of new, very specialized vocabulary. Our textbook is one resource, but when you are learning entirely new content, you need more than one resource. You need more than one way of interacting with that content. So I had my students visit *Biology4Kids.com* and *neok12.com* so that they could have more interactions with the concepts related to photosynthesis, as well as the key vocabulary.
>
> In order to fully understand photosynthesis, you need to understand plant anatomy. Considering the leaf alone, this means learning terms like *xylem* and *phloem, lower epidermis, upper epidermis, guard cells,* and *stoma.* For kids to acquire this new vocabulary, they need repetition, but not rote repetition. They need the kind of practice that requires them to think about the term, what the term means, and how the term relates to the bigger idea of photosynthesis. Internet sources can provide this type of practice in the form of games or manipulation activities. And unlike a paper–pencil exercise, it is usually fairly fast-paced; usually provides immediate and specific feedback with a chance to correct errors; and can be done in groups, in pairs, or individually, which gives me flexibility in how I incorporate it into the daily schedule.

Not only do new technologies offer new ways to engage students with traditional academic vocabulary; they broaden the landscape of academic vocabulary to be learned. The domain-specific words *desktop, icon, drop-down menu, scroll, click,* and *double-click* have very specific meanings with respect to new technologies, as do more general academic terms such as *locate, search, analyze,* and *evaluate* when these are applied to digital text. In this chapter, we address both sides of academic vocabulary as related to new technologies. First, we consider the ways in which new technologies can help students engage with academic vocabulary in ELA, social studies, mathematics, and science. Then we consider technology/digital media as a domain in and of itself, with its own academic vocabulary for students to learn. We conclude this chapter by listing resources to support teachers at all levels of technology integration, from novice to highly experienced.

THE ROLE OF NEW TECHNOLOGIES IN THE CLASSROOM

Technology holds an interesting place in many school curricula. Despite the fact that the Enhancing Education Through Technology section of the No Child Left Behind (NCLB) legislation includes directives "to improve student academic achievement through the use of technology" and "to assist every student in crossing the digital divide by ensuring that every student is technologically literate by the time the student finishes the eighth grade, regardless of race, ethnicity, gender, family income, geographic location, or disability" (U.S. Department of Education, 2001), new technologies and the skills, strategies, and language needed to use them effectively have taken a back seat to reading, writing, and mathematics. However, an underlying assumption of the CCSS (NGA & CCSSO, 2010) is that reading, writing, and research in both print and digital realms are integral aspects of today's curriculum. In fact, the CCSS suggest that as early as grade 2, students should be able to do the following:

- Analyze how visual and multimedia elements contribute to the meaning, tone, or beauty of a text (e.g., graphic novel, multimedia presentation of fiction, folktale, myth, poem). (Reading Standards, p. 12)
- Use technology, including the Internet [with support from adults], to produce and publish writing as well as to interact and collaborate with others. (Writing Standards, p. 21)
- Include multimedia components and visual displays (e.g., graphics, sound) in presentations when appropriate to enhance the development of main ideas or themes. (Speaking and Listening Standards, p. 24)

And the introductory pages of the CCSS state:

> To be ready for college, workforce training, and life in a technological society, students need the ability to gather, comprehend, evaluate, synthesize, and report on information and ideas, to conduct original research in order to answer questions or solve problems, and to analyze and create a high volume and extensive range of print and nonprint texts in media forms old and new. (p. 4)

The National Educational Technology Standards for Students (International Society for Technology in Education, 2007) identify six specific domains of technological competence: (1) creativity and innovation; (2) communication and collaboration; (3) research and information fluency; (4) critical thinking, problem solving, and decision making; (5) digital citizenship; and (6) technology operations and concepts.

When new technologies are integrated into disciplinary instruction, students are offered new ways to learn academic vocabulary while simultaneously engaging with digital tools in ways that are increasingly required in high school, college, and beyond. With this in mind, it is important to know that "the digital divide" continues. Leu and colleagues (2009) highlight the fact that classrooms with more affluent students tend to have greater technology resources than do classrooms with students in poverty. Furthermore, higher-achieving students within a classroom often have more opportunities to engage with new technologies, and engage with them for higher-level purposes, than do lower-achieving students. Therefore, we approach technology integration with an eye toward full inclusion of all students, in the recognition that academic success requires opportunities to use technology tools and communication platforms in strategic ways that go beyond basic skill practice (Celano & Neuman, 2010). In the next section, we consider specific characteristics of new technologies that are in alignment with characteristics of effective vocabulary instruction.

USING NEW TECHNOLOGIES TO SUPPORT EFFECTIVE VOCABULARY INSTRUCTION

New technologies offer tremendous possibilities for meeting the individual needs of a wide variety of students in the acquisition of new vocabulary. Digital texts often include embedded word meaning resources, such as hyperlinks to word pronunciations and definitions, and visual displays related to word meaning. This "just in time" access to both a definition and an image can prevent students from losing comprehension and engagement in the subject matter at hand. In addition, numerous software applications have been designed specifically to address concept knowledge in science, social studies, mathematics, and ELA. Other features of new technologies that can enhance vocabulary learning include the following.

Current, Authentic, Real-World Sources

It has long been acknowledged that textbooks alone are insufficient for in-depth learning in the content areas. Over the years, research has indicated that content-area texts are often inadequately written; moreover, because of their cost, they are often updated infrequently. In addition to the fact that Internet sources can be updated more easily and more frequently than can print sources, they are often primary rather than secondary sources. Instead of, or in addition to, reading what a textbook author has to say about research conducted by the National Aeronautics and Space Administration (NASA), students can make a direct visit to NASA online (*www.nasa.gov*). Instead of, or in addition to, doing textbook experiments meant to simulate real-world scientific work, students can visit the American Museum of Natural History online (*www.amnh.org*) to follow the activities of scientists engaged in current research. They might even contribute data by doing tests in their own region to complement the data collected in other regions of the world. This up-to-the-minute dimension of new technologies is one of the features that can enhance learning.

Expanded Contexts for Learning

One of the difficulties with academic language is that it is often *decontextualized*: It refers to people, objects, or events that are not physically present, and it may be conceptually abstract. Yet providing meaningful contextual information about new words and concepts is a critical component of effective instruction. The Internet and other new technologies provide a broader base of options when it comes to contextualizing domain-specific ideas and words. Imagine learning about the abstract concept of photosynthesis by viewing a variety of age-appropriate diagrams, watching videos, and hearing same-age peers around the world explain the concept in their own words.

Inherent Opportunities for Interaction

A key feature of new technologies is the degree to which they are interactive. In fact, given the same website and freedom to navigate, it is unlikely that any two people would interact with the text in the same way. Multiple hyperlink options and the ability to scroll down a webpage in seconds mean that a reader can essentially create his or her own experience with the text—determining what is viewed, the order in which it is viewed, and how it is viewed (Coiro, 2005). One way to interact with the text in service of vocabulary learning is to click on a word and instantly access a page displaying its definition. Another is to play games requiring academic vocabulary and content knowledge, such as Label the Civil Rights Movement Timeline (*www.neok12.com/diagram/Civil-Rights-Movement-01.htm*), which requires students to match key events to photographs on a timeline. In such ways, new technologies offer the capacity for increased cognitive interaction with new concepts and terms.

Multiple Modes of Receiving Information and Demonstrating Understanding

In addition to offering interactive texts, new technologies include embedded multimedia elements such as sound, photos/other still images, and video, which can be accessed instantly as desired. With careful planning and explicit instruction on how and when to use these elements, digital technologies offer rich possibilities for customized learning. In keeping with principles of differentiated instruction (Tomlinson, 2001), new technologies can be used to vary the way in which students learn, as well as the way in which they demonstrate learning. Instead of copying a definition from the dictionary, students can demonstrate genuine word knowledge by manipulating words, images, and sound. The interactive and multimedia elements of new technologies can be used to increase cognitive engagement with new words. Furthermore, several sites have different levels built into them and will adjust the level of difficulty according to students' responses.

Novel Opportunities for Practice

We cannot overemphasize the importance of repeated exposure in a variety of contexts over time for solidifying vocabulary knowledge. In addition to the engaging practice opportunities incorporated into existing websites (games, word searches, puzzles, etc.), webbing software, wikis, blogs, and podcasts allow teachers and students to record (visually, auditorily, or both) definitions, contextual information, and semantic relationships in ways that can be utilized and expanded upon over time—within a multiweek unit of study, or across years. In addition, the "just in time" supports provided by hyperlinks to definitions in the midst of online reading remove a barrier to extended practice and allow access to definitional information within the context of, but without interrupting, the reading selection.

Given this array of possibilities, we now consider just a sample of the ways in which technology can be effectively integrated into disciplinary instruction to enhance academic vocabulary knowledge.

INCORPORATING TECHNOLOGY IN THE TEACHING OF INDIVIDUAL WORDS AND CONCEPTS

Digital Field Trips

As you know, learning academic vocabulary is tightly linked with concept development and the expansion of semantic relationships among words. Third-grade teacher Ms. Barnes-Smith regularly takes her students on digital field trips to experience and interact with the academic terms and concepts of science. In a recent unit focused on ecosystems, Ms. Barnes-Smith took her students on a guided tour of a portion of the *neok12.com* website, with visits to specific pages aligned with her instructional objectives. Since this website includes links to appropriate YouTube videos, interactive games using domain-specific terms, and over 100 free images for students to use in presentations and reports, Ms. Barnes-Smith's field trip was contained within this website. She created a "trip advisory" directing the students to various webpages on the site, in a particular order. Explicit guides such as this support students in learning to navigate websites, including locating the appropriate links to move from page to page within a site. Dalton and Grisham (2011) suggest using Trackstar (*trackstar.4teachers.org*) to create the journey for students. This is especially helpful in assisting students to move from site to site, as it allows teachers to collect and annotate a series of websites for students to follow. WebQuests such as those described by Ikpeze and Boyd (2007) can also provide students with meaningful digital journeys. Experiences such as these not only provide exposure to new words and concepts; they provide interactive experiences with this new vocabulary, which in turn support in-depth learning and retention.

Podcasts

Podcasts consist of published media that can be played back on a computer or a portable device such as an iPod. Podcasts can include both audio and visual elements, and can be created by teachers and students as ways to share knowledge. Putnam and Kingsley (2009) used many of the principles of effective vocabulary instruction described in Chapter 3 to develop podcasts focused on science vocabulary for fifth graders. They found that students who accessed the podcasts in addition to participating in classroom instruction made significantly greater gains in word knowledge than did students who participated in classroom instruction alone. Students reported increased motivation to learn the vocabulary and expressed higher levels of engagement with the words. The podcasts included definitions as well as opportunities for active cognitive engagement (e.g., directions to mentally complete a sentence with a missing vocabulary word), and could be accessed by students and their parents outside of school.

At Willowdale Elementary School in Omaha, Nebraska, podcasting allows students across the grades to share word and concept knowledge. Here students demonstrate academic content knowledge on topics such as the U.S. Constitution, the American Revolution, energy, and volcanoes, while simultaneously engaging in sophisticated speaking skills associated with ELA. One podcast features five second graders discussing "Amazing Art," including interesting facts about the artists Monet, Degas, and van Gogh, as well as "Vocabulary Theater," in which they share understandings about the terms *salon, Impressionism*, and *texture* as related to these artists.

Multimedia

Original songs, published lyrics, and original artwork/photography, as well as free images available online, can be used to share conceptual knowledge; there are many fine examples of this type of sharing in postings on YouTube. For example, both teachers and students have posted short videos exploring literary devices such as *simile, metaphor, personification, hyperbole, alliteration,* and *onomatopoeia* as they occur in their everyday lives through popular songs. Often groups of students have worked together to create sophisticated representations of their concept knowledge, making connections to their prior knowledge. In a similar vein, Marcus (2008) describes the benefits of incorporating iPods into his middle school English classes, to facilitate the study of themes in literature by connecting them to themes in lyrics and quotes.

INCORPORATING TECHNOLOGY IN THE TEACHING OF STRATEGIES FOR INDEPENDENT WORD LEARNING

As discussed in Chapter 3, strategy instruction is an important component of a comprehensive vocabulary program. This instruction includes attention to resources such as dictionaries and thesauri, attention to morphology and word structure, and attention to the context within which an unfamiliar word is encountered. Online dictionaries and other digital resources that provide information about individual words are discussed in Chapter 8. Here we focus on unique ways to integrate technology into word work focused on clues within the words (structural analysis and morphology) and clues outside the words (contextual analysis), which we have introduced in Chapter 4.

Focus on Structural Analysis

Gill (2007) suggests digital graphic organizers as way to support learning about specific roots and affixes. Using webbing programs such as Kidspiration (*www.kidspiration.com*), students can create clusters of root words, prefixes, and suffixes to explore; doing this gives them a solid grasp on the meanings of roots and affixes that support content-area study. In Mrs. Bowden's third-grade classroom, students explore the prefix *multi-* as part of mathematics instruction, and return to it when they encounter words with this prefix in other content areas. Working in pairs, students create digital word clusters, including free online images and clip art. Figure 7.1 shows one such word cluster. Mrs. Bowden finds that when students manipulate the prefix with words and images, both physically and cognitively, they begin to understand how they can use this knowledge to access meanings of new words. She says:

> They hear these words all the time: *multiply, multiple, multitask,* even *multivitamin!* But it is when we do an activity like this that they stop and think about the components of these words, and [they realize] how they can now figure out the word *multicultural* when we read it in social studies, or *multilingual* when we talk about the fact that one student's mom speaks three languages!

Using the same technique with older students in a whole-class setting, Mr. Reardon's social studies class explores the root word *liber,* meaning "free." Mr. Reardon has created his own word web and saved it within a Prezi presentation to share with his class. This allows him to control the pace at which he moves through the word web, stopping for discussion throughout.

MR. REARDON: OK, everybody, I want to start class today by talking about a fundamental concept we encounter in our study of history. And for those of you taking Latin, this'll be easy. What does this Latin root mean? [Clicks to show the word *liber* in the center bubble.]

JEFF: I think it means "free."

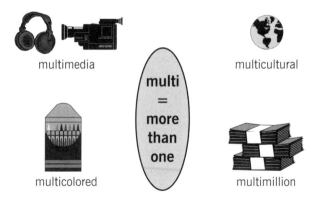

FIGURE 7.1. Digital word cluster.

MR. REARDON: Very good, Jeff. *Liber* is a Latin word that means "free," as in *liberty*. How many of you know what the word *liberty* means? [All hands go up.] So you knew some Latin even if you didn't know you knew it! *Liber* is the root word in the word *liberty*, which we hear a lot in this country. Where do you hear the word *liberty* in this country?

JUANITA: The Statue of Liberty.

CRAIG: "Give me liberty or give me death!"

TOM: The Pledge of Allegiance. "With liberty and justice for all."

MR. REARDON: Excellent. The examples you've given are even better than the ones I would have used because they show not only that we encounter the word *liberty* a lot in this country, but that we encounter it in cornerstones of our history—our pledge to our country's flag, and the statue that represented America to so many immigrants who came to Ellis Island. This idea of liberty is actually a fundamental, core principle in our country. But it is also a core idea in much of the history of the world. We in America aren't the only ones who have sought freedom and want to protect freedom. Throughout history and still today, much of the conflict in the world revolves around a desire for freedom. And so we get words like *liberate*, *liberation*, and *liberalism*. Ever hear the word *liberal*? Well, we hear it used today to refer to people with particular political interests, but the roots of this word come from the word *liberalism*.

After this whole-class activity, Mr. Reardon gives each student the task of finding a representation, in words, pictures, or audio, of the root *liber* to contribute to a class multimedia web. This web will be used throughout the school year in relation to the study of world history.

INCORPORATING TECHNOLOGY IN THE PROVISION OF RICH AND VARIED LANGUAGE EXPERIENCES

Clearly, new technologies offer new experiences with language, both written and oral. Dalton and Grisham (2011) suggest digital text as one way to increase reading volume, thereby increasing overall exposure to words. Furthermore, the Internet offers a wealth of engaging informational text, which is important in both the early and the intermediate grades (Duke, 2004). Time for Kids (*www.timeforkids.com*) and Weekly Reader (*www.weeklyreader.com*) provide high-quality online reading experiences for students; additional suggestions are provided at the end of this chapter (see Figures 7.2–7.5 on pp. 139–140). In addition to providing a wide range of reading experiences for students, it is important to provide a wide range of listening and speaking experiences to promote vocabulary growth. Many websites offer stories and informational text read aloud.

MOVING FROM RECEPTIVE TO EXPRESSIVE VOCABULARY KNOWLEDGE

The ultimate goal of vocabulary instruction is for students to "own" the words they are learning—to know them in such depth that they can use them accurately and easily in writing and conversation. Just as new technologies offer students multiple modes of receiving information about words, they offer multiple modes of expressing information about words. Students can use visuals and audio materials both to process word meanings and to demonstrate their understanding of them. An added benefit is that once created, these expressions can serve as enduring work samples or artifacts of learning, and can also serve as resources for others. Here are some ideas for encouraging students to express their word knowledge.

Thematic Glossaries

At the close of a thematic unit of study, students can create their own glossaries to highlight key academic terms and their meanings. Constructed individually or in groups, these glossaries may be posted on a secure school site for use by others in the school, or posted for use by others across the country. Among the benefits of the ability to share information with others online are the authenticity of the audience and the associated understanding that credibility and accuracy are paramount.

Wikis

A *wiki* is a collaborative site on which multiple users share and, if desired, edit content. Wikis provide a forum for processing together about new ideas and new words. For example, a visit to *mathconnections.wikispaces.com* allows students to experience definitions of geometry terms such as *cube* and *angle*, by viewing posts that include photographs and voicethreads to describe the term. They can also post their own definitions. Another useful wiki devoted to mathematics is the K–7 Mathcasts 500 Project (*http://math247.pbworks.com/w/page/20517538/K-7%20Mathcasts%20500%20Project*).

Blogs

Blogs, or online journals, allow students to write about what they are learning in a content area. In a third-grade classroom, Mrs. Thomas incorporates blogs into her literature discussion groups. She finds that it engages her students differently than face-to-face discussions do, and that a combination of the two works well for thinking about books and developing expressive skills in writing and speaking. With each book, she focuses on a particular literary element such as characterization, setting, problem, or resolution. That week, students are instructed to incorporate the term for that element into their blogs, as a way of developing precision in conversation about books and in word choice when writing and speaking. Student blogs are accessible only to students and parents in her classroom. Lubinsky (2010) suggests math blogs as a way to encourage processing of mathematics concepts and words.

INCORPORATING VOCABULARY INSTRUCTION IN THE INTERNET SEARCH PROCESS

Much has been written about the complexity of gathering and making sense of online information. In fact, many teachers have shared with us that one of the reasons they don't incorporate the Internet in their instruction as often as they could is because of the time it takes to locate valuable resources and determine how to use them effectively in the classroom. The same is true for students. Recent research illustrates the need for students to use higher-order strategies in order to navigate the Internet effectively. Specifically, they need to be able to locate information, evaluate it critically to determine the credibility and usefulness of what is found, and synthesize it across multiple sources of information (Coiro, 2005; Henry, 2006; Leu et al., 2008). Navigating to locate information is closely tied to word knowledge. Effective Internet searches require precision in the use of search terms, and this fact can also be used to improve academic vocabulary. The importance of specificity becomes very clear when students need information for a research project and do not use specific search terms. Below we provide guidelines for conducting effective Internet searches that we believe are aligned with strong academic vocabulary knowledge. These guidelines are among those described by Eagleton and Guinee (2002) as cited in Henry (2006).

1. Be specific: Narrow your focus.
2. Be exact: Use the words or phrases you hope to find.
3. Be succinct: Eliminate unnecessary words.
4. Be concise: Select key words mindfully.

For students, the process of narrowing their search terms, in concert with teacher scaffolding, can become a simultaneous process of refining word knowledge.

NEW TECHNOLOGIES, NEW MEDIA, AND NEW ACADEMIC VOCABULARY

At the beginning of this chapter, we have suggested that new technologies not only support learning of academic vocabulary within the long-standing domains of social studies, mathematics, science, and ELA, but also open a new domain of vocabulary to be learned. In this section, we discuss ways in which new technologies have changed our language and what these mean for vocabulary instruction.

New Technologies and New Literacies

The *Handbook of Research on New Literacies* (Coiro, Knobel, Lankshear, & Leu, 2008), a volume over 1,300 pages in length, is dedicated to the impact of the digital age on literacy learning. The editors of this handbook argue that digital technologies require a new set of literacy skills and strategies—multiple sets of skills and strategies, in fact—to accommodate the multimodal, multifaceted nature of new technologies. Leu, Leu, and Coiro (2004) have described these new literacies this way:

> The new literacies of the Internet include the skills, strategies, and dispositions necessary to successfully use and adapt to rapidly changing information and communication technologies and contexts that continuously emerge in our world and influence all areas of our personal and professional lives. These new literacies allow us to use the Internet and other ICTs to identify important questions, navigate to locate information, critically evaluate the usefulness of that information, synthesize information to solve problems, and communicate the solutions to others. (p. 421)

Given the centrality of technology in our world today, it is clearly a domain in and of itself, with its own vocabulary, habits of mind, and ways of operating. As with all vocabulary, the vocabulary associated with new technologies represents technology tools as well as the processes we engage in with new technologies. And because a hallmark of new technologies is the rapid rate at which they change, the related vocabulary also changes at a rapid rate. So one of the dispositions we need to foster in our students is the disposition for acquiring new language on a regular basis to reflect the ever-changing world in which we live. Table 7.1 provides just a sample of the types of academic words associated with new

TABLE 7.1. Academic Vocabulary for Using Technology Effectively

Important word types	Examples	Purposes for which these words are used
Words associated with hardware	*computer, mouse, screen, hard drive, CD, DVD, mobile device, flash drive*	To describe technology tools and devices.
Words associated with word processing and graphics software	*menu bar, drop-down menu, tool bar, desktop, icon, point, click, drag, save, file, document, scroll*	To describe and engage in the process of using and interacting with software.
Words associated with the Internet and associated software	*World Wide Web, website, webpage, search engine, Internet search, surfing the Web, navigate, browser, URL, hyperlink, posting, blog, wiki, application ("app"), download*	To describe and engage in the process of using and interacting with text online.

technologies and digital media. We will not be surprised if your students can define these better than you can!

What is fascinating about the academic vocabulary associated with new technologies is that it is in constant motion—changing as rapidly as the new technologies with which they are associated. It thus provides a strong forum for teaching students about the ways in which our language and vocabulary reflect the times and culture within which we live. There are also opportunities to discuss multiple-meaning words such as *menu, icon, search,* and *navigate,* as well as word origins. The word *podcast,* for example began as a combination of the words *iPod* and *broadcast.* Over time, and with the ability to access podcasts on a wider variety of devices, *podcast* came to stand for "<u>p</u>ortable <u>o</u>n-<u>d</u>emand broad<u>cast</u>ing" (Lubinsky, 2010). The word *blog* is a shortened version of the original *weblog.* Both *podcast* and *blog* function as both nouns and verbs, and the words *podcaster* and *blogger* refer to those who engage in podcasting and blogging, respectively.

Just as students require intentional and explicit instruction in the processes associated with new technologies, so too do they require intentional instruction in the associated vocabulary. In Chapter 4, we have described a second-grade teacher who uses instructional coaching routines to introduce new vocabulary associated with computer use. At all grade levels, it is important to use the academic language of technology with students and to require them to use the vocabulary as they work with the technology. Although students often have greater intuitive knowledge about how to operate new technologies than teachers do, research indicates that they do not possess knowledge about how to use technology for academic purposes (Zhang & Duke, 2011). Learning the academic vocabulary of new technologies is one way to reinforce instruction in the academic use of new technologies. Leu and colleagues (2004) suggest that the teacher's role is more important, not less, when technology is incorporated into instruction. With this in mind, we offer the following guidelines to support your work with new technologies and academic vocabulary instruction.

• *Start with recommended sites and recommended approaches.* In order to maximize time spent on planning and instruction, consult resources to learn about sites that would be good starting points. At the end of this chapter, Figures 7.2–7.5 list recommended sites, as well as resources to keep you up to date on recommended sites as they emerge.

• *Test the site, test the approach, and make careful selections.* Even within a recommended site, you will need to explore before deciding how best to utilize the resource within your own instructional context. Once you know what is offered, what works well, and what doesn't, you can make informed implementation decisions based on your students' needs and your instructional goals.

• *Monitor student progress and student engagement.* Once you've made an informed implementation decision, it is vitally important to observe and gauge the degree to which the new technologies are supporting student learning. Pay attention to how your students interact with the technology, where they get confused, and how they do or do not solidify their vocabulary learning as a result.

• *Provide learning guides.* Remember that your students are likely to need guidance in how best to use these new technologies. Model the ways in which students should interact with the technologies; provide guides to support their independent or group work; and incorporate instructional coaching (either by you, by a paraprofessional, or by other students) to provide scaffolding along the way.

• *Harness technology support.* If you are new to the integration of a particular technology, arrange to have a technology support person (who may be a fellow teacher) available at the start of your lesson. This resource person can often help if problems occur, and with growing experience, you will find yourself less dependent upon him or her.

• *Prepare a Plan B.* New technologies are susceptible to "going down" at inopportune times. Sometimes, in spite of careful planning and field testing, an Internet connection or an application will fail when you need it most. Therefore, it is always wise to have a backup plan in place, just in case. In such cases, you may also find a unique learning opportunity, as you problem-solve with your students to alleviate the problem. Such problem solving often requires descriptive language and the academic vocabulary of new technologies.

RESOURCES TO SUPPORT TECHNOLOGY INTEGRATION ACROSS THE SCHOOL DAY

The websites listed in Figures 7.2–7.5 offer support to extend the suggestions provided in this chapter. Most of these websites are free to use; a few require a subscription fee. Many of the suggestions in these figures appear in the book *High-Tech Teaching Success!: A Step-by-Step Guide to Using Innovative Technology in Your Classroom*, edited by Kevin Besnoy and Lane Clarke. Others appear in Brigid Dalton and Dana Grisham's (2011) article "eVoc Strategies: 10 Ways to Use Technology to Build Vocabulary," published in *The Reading Teacher*. These are both excellent sources of information, and we recommend them for further professional development.

WikiMatrix
www.wikimatrix.org

Educational Wikis
http://educationalwikis.wikispaces.com

Cool Tools for Schools
http://cooltoolsforschools.wikispaces.com/Audio+Tools

Google Earth Lesson Ideas
http://gelessons.com/lessons

FIGURE 7.2. Websites to support teacher planning and development (including wikis and podcasts).

Math Connections
http://mathconnections.wikispaces.com

K–7 Mathcasts 500 Project
http://math247.pbworks.com/w/page/20517538/K-7%20 Mathcasts%20500%20Project

Google Earth
http://earth.google.com

Explore Learning
www.explorelearning.com

Discovery Education
http://school.discoveryeducation.com

Time for Kids
www.timeforkids.com

Weekly Reader
www.weeklyreader.com

National Geographic Kids
http://kids.nationalgeographic.com/kids

Science News for Kids
www.sciencenewsforkids.org

United Nations Cyberschoolbus
http://cyberschoolbus.un.org

FIGURE 7.3. Websites to support student learning and teacher development (including wikis and podcasts).

Benjamin Franklin Tercentenary *www.benfranklin300.org*	**San Francisco Museum of Modern Art** *www.sfmoma.org*
Colonial Williamsburg *www.history.org/kids*	**Smithsonian National Air and Space Museum** *http://nasm.si.edu*
The Exploratorium's The Science of Music *www.exploratorium.edu/music*	**Smithsonian National Museum of African Art** *http://africa.si.edu*
The Field Museum *http://fieldmuseum.org*	**Smithsonian National Museum of American History** *http://americanhistory.si.edu*
John F. Kennedy Presidential Library and Museum *www.jfklibrary.org*	**Smithsonian National Museum of Natural History** *http://mnh.si.edu*
The Louvre *www.louvre.fr/en/homepage*	**Smithsonian National Postal Museum** *http://postalmuseum.si.edu*
The Monticello Classroom *http://monticello.classroom.org*	**Smithsonian National Zoological Park** *http://nationalzoo.si.edu*
The Museum of Modern Art *www.moma.org*	**The Sterling and Francine Clark Art Institute** *www.clarkart.edu*
National Aeronautics and Space Administration (NASA) *www.nasa.gov*	**Victoria and Albert Museum** *www.vam.ac.uk*

FIGURE 7.4. Museum websites and interactive museum exhibits. Adapted from Watts Taffe and Bauer (2013). Copyright 2013 by The Guilford Press. Adapted by permission.

Wordle—word cloud generated by written text *www.wordle.net*	**Bubbl.us**—mind map creator *https://bubbl.us*
Toondoo—comic strip generator *www.toondoo.com*	**PhotoPeach**—slide show creator *http://photopeach.com/about*
Glogster—site for creating interactive posters *www.glogster.com*	**Prezi**—cloud-based presentation software *http://prezi.com*
CoolText—graphic generator *http://cooltext.com*	**Inspiration** *www.inspiration.com*
Avidemux—free video editor *http://avidemux.sourceforge.net*	**Kidspiration** *www.kidspiration.com*
Diigo—personal information management system that allows students to highlight text on a webpage, attach sticky notes to it, and discuss it via threaded discussion *www.diigo.com*	**Photo Story** *www.microsoft.com/windows/using/ digitalphotography/PhotoStory/default.mspx* **iMovie** *www.apple.com/illife/imovie*
Idroo—online educational whiteboard *www.idroo.com*	

FIGURE 7.5. Digital tools for written, graphic, and video communication. Adapted from Watts Taffe and Bauer (2013). Copyright 2013 by The Guilford Press. Adapted by permission.

CONCLUDING THOUGHTS

In this chapter, we have addressed a variety of ways to utilize new technologies in teaching the meanings of specific academic words, providing strategy instruction, and immersing students in rich and varied language experiences. We have also noted that a new domain of academic vocabulary has emerged from new 21st century technologies, thus expanding the landscape of academic vocabulary. In the next chapter, we present a breadth of resources for developing academic vocabulary across the curriculum.

DISCUSSION QUESTIONS

1. There is wide variation in teachers' inclinations toward technology use in the classroom. Think about and discuss your own disposition toward the use of technology in general, and in your teaching more specifically. In what ways does this disposition pose challenges or provide strengths with respect to technology integration?

2. As discussed in this chapter, an underlying assumption of the CCSS is that technology will be incorporated into reading, writing, listening, and speaking. Discuss the expectations in the CCSS for ways in which students will be able to use digital text and multimedia text. What are you currently doing that supports students in reaching these expectations? What new ideas have you gleaned from this chapter?

3. Throughout this chapter, and especially in Figures 7.2–7.5, we reference several websites that can be incorporated into your vocabulary instruction. Select two or three of these and spend some time browsing the sites. Discuss ideas for enhancing vocabulary instruction by using some of the features you encounter.

CHAPTER 8

Resources for Developing Academic Vocabulary

In our previous chapters, we have described perspectives on academic vocabulary and given many authentic examples of classroom instruction across curricular areas. As we have developed these ideas with teachers and in classrooms, we have been asked numerous questions about instruction, but also about tools that can help teachers plan instruction and that can make learning academic vocabulary richer, deeper, and more engaging for students. This chapter presents our answers to some of the questions we are asked as we visit classrooms and collaborate with teachers who want to share ideas. These questions are as follows:

- How can we choose words for content instruction?
- How many words should I teach?
- What are good resource references for K–8 students?
- What other media resources and games are useful for student word learning?
- What about assessment?
- What kind of leadership ensures vibrant vocabulary instruction in our schools?

CHOOSING WORDS FOR CONTENT-AREA INSTRUCTION

Teachers know that students have a right to be instructed on key content-area vocabulary, but sometimes feel unsure about selecting the most important vocabulary to be learned. Beck and colleagues (2013) have been leaders in promoting the idea of three tiers of word importance. As described in earlier chapters of this book, Tier Three words are unfamiliar words for specific concepts (e.g., *photosynthesis*) that need extended time and effort for instruction in content-area classes; Tier Two words are words that are new labels for established concepts (e.g., *petal*); and Tier One words are the most basic words (*flower, leaf*) that usually do not require instruction in school for students whose are comfortable with English as the language of instruction.

Choosing content words is facilitated by the textual materials that are used in many classrooms. Boldface, highlighting, and glossaries help with this selection process. The frequency of a term's occurrence also provides a clue to its importance, as does its use in diagrams/figures and in labeling. The CCSS (NGA & CCSSO, 2010) highlight the need for students to develop the ability to select their own words for learning in the content areas, as in the following reading standard for informational text:

5. Use text features and search tools (e.g., key words, sidebars, hyperlinks) to locate information relevant to a given topic efficiently. (p. 14)

Carol Clay, the third-grade two-way immersion (English and Spanish) teacher we have met in Chapter 6, helps her students learn how to select vocabulary for study using typography and frequency. In a recent unit, students selected informational books on sound from the classroom sets. Their assignment was to skim to locate three to five words in each chosen book that they believed would be important to the unit and should be learned. They were to write these words on sticky notes to bring to the large-group discussion. Carol prepared her students for this activity by teaching a mini-lesson on typographical clues and word frequency, to help the students select appropriate words from the books. She also introduced them to the academic vocabulary—for instance, *text feature*, *boldface*, and *frequency*. She concluded her mini-lesson by stating, "You need to use *text features* to pick out important vocabulary. If a word is in *boldface* and is *frequent*, or occurs many times, then it is probably an important word."

When the large group reconvened, one student began by placing one sticky note on the chart, and then other students who had chosen the same word followed suit. In this way, the class constructed a chart of important terms (the most frequent words on their sticky notes). This gave them experience in selecting critical academic vocabulary, which is a valuable study skill. Carol could also add words she believed were important if the students did not contribute them to the chart (see Figure 6.8 on p. 117).

Charlene Cobb, a district reading coordinator, supported her teachers in working together to select words across the grades. Her method was to have each grade choose 100 words for study during the year in each content area. Teachers at each grade level came together to compile a list of words from their textbooks that were identified as words for instruction. They worked as a team to identify the most essential words for instruction, and organized their list to match the sequence of the curriculum. This collaborative process also had an interesting effect on parents who sometimes felt that the curriculum differed dramatically from teacher to teacher. The teachers' team decision making communicated to the parents the integrity of the content-area instruction across different classrooms; it also allowed parents to know and reinforce the vocabulary at home, if and when they could.

Baumann and Graves (2010, p. 8) provide a similar model for selecting math vocabulary:

> First, identify the domain-specific words at an appropriate level (e.g., a middle school math teacher would work from Marzano and Pickering's Level 3 math list, which corresponds to grades 6–8). Second, identify words deemed to be important for instruction (e.g., words from the Level 3 math list that appear in the adopted math textbook, curriculum, or state standards). Third, select words for instruction by asking, "Is this term critically important to the mathematics content I will be teaching this year?" .. . Fourth, organize the selected words according to how they occur in your curriculum.

To cross-check, teachers can use word lists such as those created by Marzano and Pickering (2005) or Harris and Jacobson (1982) to help them in constructing lists of high-utility content words.

DECIDING HOW MANY WORDS TO TEACH

The question of how many words to teach is a tricky one that is relatively unexamined in the research literature, partly because there is so much variation in the prior knowledge of students in every classroom. Graves (2006) estimates that there is a 3,000-word difference between the entering vocabularies of the most knowledgeable and least knowledgeable kindergarteners—a gap that grows larger across the grades. This difference in learners is only one aspect of the difficulty of this question.

We also need to acknowledge the differing utility of unknown words. For example, the text for a science unit on sound contains the vocabulary word *pinnae* (the visible portions of the ear that project from the head). It's a word that most adults do not know, and it does not have high utility in helping the students understand the key issues of how sound is produced. This is therefore a low-utility word, and even though it is unknown, it should not be high on the list of key vocabulary for special focus

In that same unit, the term *vibration* is essential, as is *waveform*. Without an understanding of these two terms, the production of sound is incomprehensible. These are "everybody" words. All students need to understand these words and to be able to use them in their speech, writing, and other expressive endeavors (such as lab work and lab reports) if they are to understand sound; they also need to understand the concepts of *vibration* and *waveform* in other contexts.

A third consideration in how many words to teach is how hard words are to teach. Some terms are simple synonyms for related concepts; if you have seen a wave, you can understand *waveform* without too much instruction.

We have a three-word mnemonic for vocabulary teaching: *Flood, Fast, Focus.*

Flood

First, *Flood* your classroom with words related to your topic of study, not all of which you want your students to learn to the same depth. You want them to have seen and heard these words, such as *pinnae*, and relate them to the general topical category. They can create word blasts or semantic maps, and engage in sorting and other playful activities, to begin building a relational net of terms related to sound. Students can select their own words for personal word books or word walls/wizards to begin recording their own interesting words. This allows your students with more prior knowledge to stretch their knowledge, but it also allows students who are just building a basic vocabulary to choose the Fast and Focus words for their study goals. You can have as many Flood words as you want in a class to enrich the environment, but these are not assigned to all or tested in traditional ways. Rather, they form a backdrop of topically related terms for incidental learning.

Fast

Use *Fast* instruction for terms like *waveform*, where an easy definition or analogy will build on knowledge the students already have. Make sure the students see the word, can pronounce it, and have a "kid-friendly" definition for the term. Often a visual or physical description helps as well. For students whose grade-level English vocabulary is still developing, follow up with extra practice and use.

Focus

Use *Focus* instruction for words like *photosynthesis*, where deeper, semantically rich teaching of a new concept is required. This is the type of conceptual instruction that takes time and energy, but it pays off with deep learning of those Tier Three words. If Fast and Focus words are "everybody" words, keep the number limited to a reasonable number, and remember to factor in words from all your content areas to make sure that students are not overloaded. You can also pretest students on unit vocabulary and assign different lists (Flood, Fast, Focus) to different students as needed.

GOOD REFERENCE RESOURCES FOR K–8 STUDENTS

In the last decade, there has been an explosion in good reference tools for K–8 students. In this section, we describe basic references—dictionaries, encyclopedias, and thesauri—in both book and online formats.

Learner Dictionaries

There are many lists of good dictionaries for our target-age students (Blachowicz & Fisher, 2010), but so many times these are not helpful because the definitions are too complex for developing readers. We have found that all students benefit from access to what are called *learner dictionaries*. These are reference tools with definitions written in clear and "student-friendly" ways—that is, with language that can be easily understood and with salient examples.

Excellent examples of learner dictionaries are the Longman Learner Dictionaries, whose clear, easily understood definitions provide access to the basic vocabulary that underpins more complex content learning. These are available at various levels, and audio CDs are also available for some of them.

Basic/Beginning

Longman Photo Dictionary of American English.—Designed for adult learners of English, this new dictionary uses clear, contemporary color photos to make new words easy to remember. Suitable for both classroom and home use, this dictionary teaches real-world language in realistic contexts to help beginners master over 3,000 key words.

Low Beginning—Low Intermediate

Longman Basic Dictionary of American English.—The clear, simple definitions in this dictionary are written with the 2,000-word Longman Defining Vocabulary, which means that students are sure to understand the explanations. Helpful, natural examples illustrate the words and phrases in typical contexts, so students learn as well as understand. The engaging cartoons and clear, open design contribute to a dictionary that students will enjoy using.

Beginning/Low Intermediate—Intermediate

Longman Study Dictionary of American English.—This new dictionary is guaranteed to help students understand difficult words and concepts, many of which are found in content-area classes. Again, every definition is written with the Longman Defining Vocabulary of the 2,000 most common words. The examples provide further explanation of the meanings, to be sure students understand and can differentiate words in the same family.

Low Intermediate

Longman Dictionary of American English, Fourth Edition.—The most recent edition of this well-regarded American English learner dictionary helps intermediate students build their vocabulary. And it now offers extra help and support for students who are studying other subjects in English.

Beginning—High Intermediate

Longman American Idioms Dictionary.—Help your students "get a handle" on all kinds of American idioms with this dictionary, which contains more than 4,000 idioms from spoken and written English. Again, these are defined with the 2,000-word Longman Defining Vocabulary.

Intermediate—Advanced

There are many other Longman Learners Dictionaries in dual languages and at differing levels of complexity (available at *www.pearsonlongman. com/ae/dictionaries/content.html*).

School Dictionaries

Along with learner dictionaries, there are many dictionaries published for the school market. Some well-regarded ones are listed below, with names of publishers if these are not included in the titles.

Beginning Dictionaries

American Heritage Picture Dictionary (Houghton Mifflin)
Good Morning Words (Scott Foresman)
Macmillan/McGraw-Hill Picture Word Book
My Pictionary (Scott Foresman)

Early Elementary School Dictionaries

Macmillan First Dictionary
My First Dictionary (Scott Foresman)
My First Picture Dictionary (Scott Foresman)
Very First Dictionary (Macmillan)
Words for New Readers (Scott Foresman)

Upper Elementary/Junior High School Dictionaries

American Heritage Children's Dictionary (Houghton Mifflin)
Childcraft Dictionary (World Book)
Gage Canadian Dictionary
Macmillan School Dictionary
Scott Foresman Intermediate Dictionary
Scribner Intermediate Dictionary
Webster's New World Children's Dictionary
World Book Student Dictionary

Advanced Dictionaries

Longman Dictionary of Contemporary English
Macmillan Dictionary for Students
Scott Foresman Advanced Dictionary
Scribner Dictionary
Thorndike-Barnhart Student Dictionary
World Book Dictionary

Content-Area References

There are also many dictionaries available for school use that focus on the content areas. The Usborne Content Dictionaries (*www.usborne.com*) are also learner dictionaries because of their clear, friendly definitions, as well as examples and graphics that deal with math, science, history, music, and other content domains. Other popular content-area dictionaries include the following:

Math Dictionary for Kids: The Essential Guide to Math Terms, Strategies, and Tables, by Theresa R. Fitzgerald. Waco, TX: Prufrock Press, 2011.
Science Dictionary for Kids: The Essential Guide to Science Terms, Concepts, and Strategies, by Laurie E. Westphal. Waco, TX: Prufrock Press, 2009.

Online Dictionaries

For many students and teachers, online dictionaries are the references of choice. Dictionary.com (*www.dictionary.com*) is the "granddaddy" of electronic resources. Other electronic tools include the following:

Word Central Merriam-Webster (*www.wordcentral.com*).—Dictionary, thesaurus, and rhyming dictionary plus games for educators; now reprogrammed for superior word power and language fun.

English Pronouncing Dictionary with Instant Sound (*www.howjsay.com*).— Here is a neat dictionary that says the word for your students! They will really like this. Well-read persons know hundreds, even thousands, of words that they've never heard anyone pronounce. Search through the 82,576 sound files and listen while somebody pronounces your chosen mystery words.

Merriam-Webster Visual Dictionary (*http://visual.merriam-webster.com*).— This visual dictionary will help your students translate words into pictures. You can browse by broad themes (Animal Kingdom, Food and Kitchen, Arts and Architecture, Science, Sports and Games, etc.). The search engine takes some getting used to: Enter your word, wait for the word to display under "Images," click on it, and hit "Go to." When the image (or images) is displayed, the theme it's part of is highlighted on the navigation bar. Sometimes detailed images that *are* there, (e.g., a pommel horse) won't show up in a search but can be accessed through the broader category they're part of (in the case of the pommel horse, gymnastics).

An advantage of an online dictionary is access to an invaluable research tool with exhaustive information, ranging from the general-purpose *Oxford Pocket Dictionary of Current English*, to social science terms in *A Dictionary of Psychology*, to health-related nutrition definitions in *A Dictionary of Food Nutrition*.

Online Encyclopedias

For content-area vocabulary, encyclopedias are often the best resources because they provide the extended context required to understand such vocabulary. Though good encyclopedias often come bundled in school computer packages, the following are also highly regarded:

DKE Encyclopedia (*www.dke-encyc.com/youandinternet.asp*).—Dorling Kindersley and Google bring you their best of the Web. Dorling

Kindersley is known for providing excellent photographs and diagrams that explicate concepts clearly.

Columbia Encyclopedia (*http://education.yahoo.com/reference/encyclopedia*).—This free online encyclopedia contains over 50,000 entries and more than 84,000 hypertext cross-references, covering a wide range of research and reference topics. The Columbia Encyclopedia is one of the most complete and up-to-date electronic encyclopedias ever produced.

Specialized Dictionaries and Encyclopedias

Who2 (*www.who2.com*).—Who2 is an encyclopedia of famous people. It includes well-researched profiles of real people, fictional characters, and some figures (like Robin Hood) who may be either. It also includes profiles of celebrities who aren't people, like Ham the Chimp and Hal 9000.

Encyclopedia of Greek and Roman Mythology (Roman & Roman, 2010).— This is a comprehensive and sophisticated compendium of Greek and Roman mythology, so much of which underlies English vocabulary. For younger students, *D'Aulaires' Book of Greek Myths* (D'Aulaire, 1962) has been in print for over 50 years, attesting to its quality and interest level.

The Cook's Thesaurus (*www.foodsubs.com*).—The Cook's Thesaurus is actually a cooking encyclopedia that covers thousands of ingredients and kitchen tools. Entries include pictures, descriptions, synonyms, pronunciations, and suggested substitutions.

Don't let your appreciation of online resources diminish your pleasure in other book references. There are many specialized content dictionaries for math and science, both in book form and online. As well, there are dictionaries and encyclopedias for every content interest, from ponies to cars to skateboards to dance. Use your search engine to find ones for your class, or turn this into an online or library browsing assignment for your students: Who can bring in the most intriguing special-interest reference?

OTHER MEDIA RESOURCES AND GAMES FOR STUDENTS

Television Programs

Word Girl and *Word World* are two animated programs (currently shown on U.S. public television) that focus on vocabulary building for elementary students. *Word Girl* (*http://pbskids.org/wordgirl*) is an alien with superpowers whose secret identity is Becky Botsford, a 10½-year-old fifth-grade student who was born on the fictional planet Lexicon. She was sent away after sneaking onto a spaceship. Each episode begins with verbal instructions to listen for two words that will be used throughout the plot of that episode. The words (examples include *diversion, cumbersome, and idolize*) are chosen according to academic guidelines and explained through words and actions. Becky's animated adventures are interspersed with game shows and other playful encounters with words. Viewers can also follow up with activities at the program's PBS Kids website (see above).

WordWorld (*www.wordworld.com*) is an Emmy Award–winning show that airs in 10 languages and in 89 countries besides the United States. The television series stars Dog and his WordFriends, a host of animals who help him on his travels. In each *WordWorld* episode, Dog undertakes a series of adventures in which the only way to save the day is to "build a word." When the word is built correctly, it transforms itself into the thing it represents, which gives instant meaning to the word.

Games for Vocabulary Development

Online Games

The Internet is awash with word games for children, teachers, and parents. The site Funbrain (*www.funbrain.com*) hosts many that can be played free of charge (see Figure 8.1).

The Read, Write, Think website (*www.readwritethink.org*), sponsored by the International Reading Association and the National Council of Teachers of English, has a number of resources for vocabulary games and instruction ideas. Students and teachers love the Crossword Puzzle Tool (*www.readwritethink.org/files/resources/interactives/crossword/crossword.swf*), which allows them to create wonderful puzzles from their academic vocabulary.

Commercial Games

Building word interest and consciousness is aided by having good word games in the classroom. We suggest Bananagrams (Edley & the Creators of Bananagrams, 2009) and Apples to Apples (Mattel Corporation, 1999) as games that stimulate interest in words for upper elementary students. Charades and Jeopardy also can be adapted for academic vocabulary learning (for the latter, see *http://jeopardylabs.com*). Other old favorites, like Scrabble, Spill and Spell, and Boggle (see the list on the next page), can help build a "game library" for your classroom or school, and most are available in online versions. Some schools keep sets of games in the school library to circulate among classes. Games for the classroom might include the following:

• Word Confusion Do you know the difference between these words?	• Stay Afloat Don't get soaked by the wrong word.
• Scramble-Saurus always I place mis my letters.	• Word Turtle Make your own word search puzzles.
• Infoplease Word of the Day Strengthen your vocabulary.	• Spellaroo Hop on the misspelled word.
• 2Bee or Nottoobee What's the buzz about being?	• Spell Check Something is wrong with one of these words.
• The Plural Girls Help the kitties pop the bubbles.	• Wacky Tales Write your own crazy story.
• Paint by Idioms Add color to your language.	• Sign the Alphabet Use your hands to communicate.
• Grammar Gorillas Monkey around with your grammar skills.	• What's the Word Read new words.
	• Translator Alligator How do you say *boca grande*?

FIGURE 8.1. Games available on the Funbrain site (*www.funbrain.com*).

Blurt!: The Webster's Game of Word Racing.—Players take turns reading a definition aloud while others blurt out guesses in a race for the right word. Ages 10–adult; includes a junior version for ages 7–9. Riverside Publishing Company, 1992.

Boggle Junior.—Players associate words with pictures and find letters on cubes that match the letters in the words. Ages 3–6. Parker Bros., 1988.

Boggle Master: 3-Minute Word Game.—Players link letters up, down, sideways, and diagonally to form words within the time limit. Ages 8 and up. Parker Bros., 1993.

Claymania.—Players draw cards with words that depict the object into which the clay must be molded within the 45-second time limit. Ages 12 and up. Classic Games, 1993.

Go to the Head of the Class (Deluxe Edition).—Players answer quiz questions that are divided into three knowledge levels and cover every subject. Ages 8–adult. Milton Bradley, 1986.

Guesstures: The Game of Split-Second Charades.—Players act out four words at a time within a given time limit. Ages 12 and up. Milton Bradley, 1990.

Hangman: The Original Word Guessing Game.—Players guess letters of their opponent's word, trying not to make incorrect guesses, each of which would expose another part of the hangman. Ages 8–adult. Milton Bradley, 1988.

Outburst Junior.—Players on a team have 60 seconds to yell out answers that fit familiar categories within a given time limit. Ages 7–14. Western Publishing, under license from Hersch and Co., 1989.

Overturn.—Players find words from randomly placed letters that must be in a continuous line in order to form the word. Ages 8–adult. Pressman Toy Corporation, 1993.

Pictionary Junior: The Classic Game of Quick Draw for Kids.—Players sketch clues for teammates, who have to quickly guess the word from the card that was drawn. Ages 8–14. Golden and Design, 1993.

Scattergories Junior.—Players draw cards that have six categories on them. They must roll the die to determine which letter their answers must begin with to fill each of the six categories. Ages 8–11. Milton Bradley, 1989.

Scrabble Crossword Game.—Players connect letter titles up and down and across the board to make words of various point values. Ages 8–adult. Milton Bradley, 1989.

Tribond Kids.—Players answer questions by using association and grouping methods to obtain the correct answer. Ages 7–11. Big Fun A Go Go, 1993.

Upwords.—A three-dimensional crossword game. Players can build new words in crossword puzzle style or by stacking tiles already on the board. Ages 10–adult. Milton Bradley, 1988.

ASSESSMENT

Earlier in this chapter, we have suggested a methodology for teacher word selection, as all assessment strategies assume a process for the selection of key vocabulary words. In the section following this one, we discuss leadership, to emphasize that every member of the school leadership community is responsible for assessment (both formative and summative). Besides large-scale standardized measures, classroom-based assessment is critical. Often this takes the form of assessments administered before and after content-area units.

In a novel approach, Charlene Cobb asked her teachers to select 100 content and academic words for focus during the school year (Cobb, 2003). The assessment process served as a preview and review of words students would be expected to learn over the course of the year. This process consisted of the following steps:

1. Each week, teachers randomly selected 10 words (the square root of the entire group of 100).
2. Each word was read aloud to the students, along with the content area to which it belonged. Students were provided with a written representation of the word, either on the board or on a worksheet.
3. As each word was read aloud, students had a brief amount of time to define it in writing, using a standard definition, example, sentence, or illustration.

4. After students completed the 10 words, the teacher read aloud the words and provided a brief description of acceptable responses. For words that had not yet been taught, teachers simply explained that these were words students would learn more about in the future.

5. Teachers collected all papers each week, scored them, and charted the learning of their students over the year. The percentage of total words correct each week for the entire class was charted on a classroom graph.

This graphing and charting sensitized both students and teachers to the key vocabulary and to the growth in the students' vocabularies. It also provided a communal word bank for all teachers at a grade level to help focus their instruction.

As we have described in Chapter 6, the teachers implementing *Vocabulary Visits* (Blachowicz & Obrochta, 2005) for a science unit on sound used their model of using a written preunit brainstorm list of topically related vocabulary by each student and a postunit brainstorm as assessments. One teacher, however, had her students do their postunit assessments as "word clouds" (see Figure 6.10) to add variety to the assessment. The teacher not only checked the growth of the relational set, but looked for students' inclusion in their word clouds of the "everybody" words noted earlier in this chapter—words the teacher had selected as key vocabulary she wanted everyone to gain from the unit. She also used the students' summaries and lab sheets to check for use of the words in writing.

In a 3-year study of vocabulary instruction (Baumann et al., 2011), Blachowicz and her colleagues (2011) used graphic organizers called *vocabulary frames* as learning scaffolds. Students were pretested on teacher-selected vocabulary deemed important for the unit. They worked as a group to make their selection of "everybody words," using guidance from their curriculum materials, from a vocabulary frequency list (Marzano & Pickering, 2005) and from their past experience. They then pretested the students by using a frame for both literary and informational narratives called a *Vocab-o-Gram* (Blachowicz & Fisher, 2010). Figure 8.2 shows a sample Vocab-o-Gram frame for the book *Keep the Lights Burning, Abbie* (Roop & Roop, 1985), a narrative about a young girl's bravery in keeping signal lights burning during a storm. After completion of the units, students were asked to summarize core selections, without any directions being given to use key vocabulary that the teachers had selected for study. Acting as their own controls, students used twice as many words correctly in their written summaries when they had completed a text frame for that selection. They also used twice as many words as a control group who did not use the frames. Their spontaneous use in writing was the assessment tool for learning.

Pre- and postunit assessment can be carried out in many other ways. Carol Clay's third-grade two-way immersion curriculum includes a unit of study on the Aztecs. Students are pretested on "everybody words," and their postunit test is the compilation of a dictionary of Aztec terms (see Figure 8.3 on page 156). This

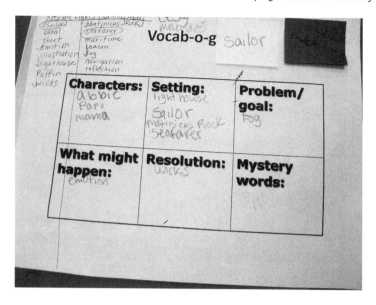

FIGURE 8.2. Vocab-o-Gram.

not only assesses the students' knowledge of the key vocabulary; it also assesses their knowledge of how dictionaries present vocabulary. Teachers in the Multi-faceted Comprehensive Vocabulary Instruction Program at Washington School in Evanston, Illinois, use crossword puzzles created with Read, Write, Think's Crossword Puzzle Tool (see "Online Games," above) for assessment. Students need to create their own puzzles of key content words, which are scored by teachers as assessments and which also provide pleasurable practice for their classmates. The possibilities are endless.

LEADERSHIP FOR ACADEMIC VOCABULARY DEVELOPMENT

All of the resources and approaches described above are effective tools when used by knowledgeable teachers in schools where there is leadership for academic vocabulary learning. Leadership is required in the district, in the school, and in the classroom. Let's look at how three professionals who work in multicultural metropolitan districts describe what's important in their educational settings.

At the District Level

Charlene Cobb, introduced earlier in this chapter, is a district executive director of teaching and learning who is responsible for curriculum and instruction for grades K–8. In her view, leadership for academic vocabulary learning has to be

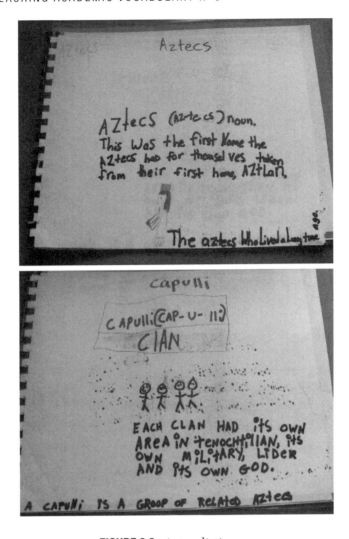

FIGURE 8.3. Aztec dictionary.

established at all levels, but the district-level leadership has the responsibility for setting district expectations for administrators. She comments:

> The most important thing a literacy director can do to provide leadership and to stimulate the teaching and learning of academic vocabulary in a district is understand the underlying needs and work with the principals to support the needs of the students and teachers. Needs are determined by examining various sources of data and understanding the school cultures related to instruction. From this, the literacy director needs to formulate goals and action plans that can be shared with principals. I have found that principal support is critical to effectively working with teachers to support

students. Getting principal buy-in is critical. The next step is providing principals with the knowledge needed to support the goals. Sometimes this can be as simple as a phone call or meeting, and other times it might mean providing presentations, discussing articles, doing a book study, or giving principals an article/book to read on their own.

The most important things a principal can do to provide leadership and to stimulate the teaching and learning of academic vocabulary in a school are very similar to what a literacy leader does in terms of understanding the underlying need. However, in order to determine need, they first need an understanding of best practices for academic vocabulary and access to resources. I've found that some principals do this almost organically; others seek the support of their reading specialists or coaches; and some search for programs that will "fix" the problem. The most powerful instances I've witnessed are when principals and teachers meet on a regular basis for professional discourse around questions such as these: What are our students' needs? What do we need to do in order to meet these needs? How will we know when we've done this? What is our plan? How will we implement and monitor this plan? These are simple sentences that lead to complex conversations.

At the School Level

Ellen Fogelberg is assistant superintendent for curriculum and operations for the elementary schools of a K–8 district. Her direct charge is to work with principals to support them in working in their schools to achieve district goals. Ellen agrees with Char's points above and adds these tips for principals:

Leadership at the district level for any initiative is as much about naming the problem and creating the conditions for others to believe in the necessity of solving the problem collectively and collaboratively as it is about providing direction. It is also about providing the resources (experts, articles and books, videos, etc.), professional development, and time for those directly involved in working on the problem to take ownership of the possible solutions. It is also about letting others take some risks in changing practice to address the identified issue.

The district literacy director often needs to work with the school administrators to understand the nature of the problem with vocabulary development and possibilities for improving vocabulary. This is important because the principals have to feel some level of comfort in addressing vocabulary as an issue worth exploring with the staff. In terms of vocabulary development, it is important for the district leaders as well as the staff to think about improving students' vocabulary as improving students' academic achievement. Vocabulary is one indicator of conceptual understanding and can easily be considered an avenue for school improvement.

Leadership for change includes developing other leaders. In addition to classroom teachers, it is helpful for the principal to think about how other staff members can support a schoolwide effort to improve vocabulary. Some of the questions to consider when developing a plan for improving students' vocabulary development include the following: Which classroom teachers have expertise in vocabulary development? What have teachers done in each of the domains to facilitate students understanding and use of academic vocabulary? What does good vocabulary instruction look like? What does student work look like when there is an emphasis on vocabulary development? These and other questions may augment the important initial questions once the staff seriously considers making vocabulary development a major effort for the year. Then the building leader can begin to find opportunities for teachers to share their work, compare student samples, and create benchmarks for evaluating the effects of their work.

Another important consideration for leaders is how to provide the resources the staff needs in terms of research, materials, time, and opportunities for evaluating and celebrating successes. Finally, district and school leaders need to consider what it will take to maintain the momentum for such an endeavor after the first year, knowing that what is needed is change in practice that is lasting. Can the staff determine 1-year goals, 3-year goals, and perhaps 5-year goals? Leadership includes facilitation skills to maintain the enthusiasm for change and understanding when bumps in implementation occur. Finally, leadership for vocabulary development includes becoming an equal partner with the staff in moving the work forward with students.

At the Classroom Level: Coaches and Consultants

Connie Obrochta is a teacher leader and literacy coach in a large multicultural school. She works with teachers and children to actualize instruction in the classroom. Connie reflects on what is needed for teacher leadership at the classroom level:

I think it's important that the PD [professional development] for the teachers is manageable and sustained, so they are taking this work to a deeper level over time through a scaffolded approach. In order for the PD to truly "take root" and make an impact on student achievement, it's important to develop and sustain a school culture where all teachers in the building are encouraged and expected to (1) regularly observe and describe their students' strengths and needs; (2) discuss and design instruction based upon those needs; and (3) regularly share with colleagues in grade-level teams and across grade levels what they have learned and what they are thinking about for next steps. I think if those systems aren't in place, there will be some strong examples happening in individual classrooms, but the power of having the whole school/district moving in a seamless direction for the children will likely be diluted.

I've come to believe that principals are the most critical component in crafting this kind of culture over time. Their presence during instructional team conversations can make or break the sustainability of this work.

Claire, a consultant who works with districts on leadership for instruction, shares this list of tips for leadership in regard to academic and content vocabulary instruction:

- Make vocabulary a school priority, and support innovative, motivational, and fun ways to build your "brand" as a vocabulary school. For example, one of our principals supported making the Halloween parade a "vocabulary parade." Teachers and students added a vocabulary word to their costumes, which gave rise to a lot of amusing conversations about words between children, parents, and other watchers. In this prioritization, emphasize that vocabulary is taught in all content areas and is everyone's responsibility.
- Make sure that your professional development is sustained long enough to make a difference. Research by the National Staff Development Council [Darling Hammond, Wei, Andree, Richardson, & Orphanos, 2009] suggests [that] at least 60 hours of professional development [are] needed to effect change.
- Organize the schedule so teachers have time to meet in grade groups and cross-grade groups for school articulation. Be sure to highlight academic and content vocabulary selection, instruction, and assessment as a goal.
- Provide support personnel to work with teachers, and encourage teachers to collaborate for mutual support, emphasizing that instructional leadership is distributed across the school and the content areas.
- Participate in teacher work groups, and work with support personnel to monitor and support group ideas.
- Provide the resources teachers need to do a good job, and make sure these are distributed across the content areas.
- Connect with other principals to share concerns, issues, and ideas.
- Spotlight the good news about vocabulary in your school to parents and the wider community.

At the Classroom Level: Teachers

Teachers in schools with effective academic and content vocabulary programs take their leadership role seriously. They lead and participate in curriculum groups; participate in peer coaching and support; and bring new ideas from their academic work, experience, and personal learning. At schools in these districts, teachers often form their own study groups to work on issues, to review the latest research and practice literature, to try out ideas in the classroom, and to reflect with one another on student performance. These are "growth groups" where they can take chances, exchange ideas, and build their capacity to lead in the classroom and in the school. There are many resources for teacher study groups in vocabulary; several books are devoted to setting up such groups, including one focused specifically on vocabulary (see Figure 8.4).

A survey of over 200 teachers attending local meetings of the International Reading Association identified the books listed in Figure 8.5 (two of which have been updated to reflect more recent editions) as useful core titles for study groups in vocabulary (Berne & Blachowicz, 2009).

Besides participating in study groups, teachers exhibit leadership when they bring the results of study to their school and district curriculum work teams, along with examples of their classroom trials. Leadership for vocabulary learning comes from all members of the school community. Teachers, principals, and district administrators must all work together to build a learning community around academic and content vocabulary.

CONCLUDING THOUGHTS

In this chapter, we have shared with you our answers to the most common teacher questions that we have encountered in our work in schools and classrooms. Teachers have asked for guidance about selecting and prioritizing vocabulary for instruction, and for assessing this new vocabulary in ways that get at students' actual ability to use it. They have also sought resources to make their instruction

---

- Cayuso, E., Fegan, C., & McAlister, D. (2004). *Designing teacher study groups: A guide for success*. Gainesville, FL: Maupin House.
- Dimino, J., & Taylor, M. (2009). *Learning how to improve vocabulary instruction through teacher study groups*. Baltimore: Brookes.
- Murphy, C., & Lick, D. (2005). *Whole-faculty study groups: Creating professional learning communities that target student learning* (3rd ed.). Thousand Oaks, CA: Corwin Press.
- Ogle, D. (2007). *Coming together as readers* (2nd ed.). Thousand Oaks, CA: Corwin Press.

FIGURE 8.4. Resources for teacher study groups in vocabulary.

- Allen, J. (1999). *Words, words, words: Teaching vocabulary in grades 4– 12*. York, ME: Stenhouse.
- Kame'enui, E. J., & Baumann, J. F. (Eds.). (2012). *Vocabulary instruction: Research to practice* (2nd ed.). New York: Guilford Press.
- Beck, I. L., McKeown, M. G., & Kucan, L. (2013). *Bringing words to life: Robust vocabulary instruction* (2nd ed.). New York: Guilford Press.
- Blachowicz, C. L. Z., & Fisher, P. (2010). *Teaching vocabulary in all classrooms* (4th ed.). Boston: Pearson/Allyn & Bacon.
- Farstrup, A., & Samuels, S. J. (Eds.). (2008). *What the research has to say about vocabulary instruction*. Newark, DE: International Reading Association.
- Ganske, K. (2000). *Word journeys*. New York: Guilford Press.
- Graves, M. F. (2006). *The vocabulary book: Learning and instruction*. New York: Teachers College Press.
- Graves, M. F. (Ed.). (2009). *Essential readings on vocabulary instruction*. Newark, DE: International Reading Association.

FIGURE 8.5. Teacher-identified core titles for study groups in vocabulary.

more engaging and relevant to students of a new millennium who are comfortable with technology in their daily lives. And we have shared our perspectives, and perspectives from the field, on the leadership needed to support teachers in their goal of making every student a capable and independent word learner and word lover across all areas of the curriculum.

DISCUSSION QUESTIONS

1. Work with your group, grade, or team to develop a protocol for choosing words for study from a chapter or selection you are using. Then try it out individually and compare the results. Critically analyze your protocol. What worked? What didn't work? How would you revise it?

2. Examine two of the dictionaries mentioned in this chapter that would be appropriate for your work. Which would work best for your students and why? What features do you want in a class dictionary for your level and why? Pool your ideas to construct a dictionary evaluation checklist.

3. Use the ideas in this chapter to develop a list of essentials for all the classrooms at your grade level. Prepare an argument you might present to an administrator explaining the need for certain resources relating to the conceptual framework described in Chapter 3 (see Figure 3.3, p. 42).

References

Achugar, M., Schleppegrell, M., & Oteiza, T. (2007). Engaging teachers in language analysis: A functional linguistics approach to reflective literacy. *English Teaching: Practice and Critique, 6*(2), 8–24.

Alverman, D. E., & Hynd, C. R. (1989). Study strategies for correcting misconceptions in physics: An intervention. In S. McCormick & J. Zutell (Eds.), *Cognitive and social perspectives for literacy research and instruction*. Thirty-eighth Yearbook of the National Reading Conference. Chicago: National Reading Conference.

Anderson, L. W., & Krathwohl, D. R. (Eds.). (2001). *A taxonomy for learning, teaching and assessing: A revision of Bloom's taxonomy of educational objectives: Complete edition*. New York: Longman.

Anderson, R. C., & Nagy, W. E. (1991). Word meanings. In R. Barr, M. Kamil, P. B. Mosenthal, & P. D. Pearson (Eds.), *Handbook of reading research* (Vol. 2, pp. 690–724). New York: Longman.

Atwater, R., & Atwater, F. (1988). *Mr. Popper's penguins*. Boston: Little, Brown.

Aukerman, M. (2007). A culpable CALP: Rethinking the conversational/academic language proficiency distinction in early literacy instruction. *The Reading Teacher, 60*, 626–634.

Avi. (1984). *The fighting ground*. New York: Lippincott.

Bailey, A. L., Butler, F. A., LaFramenta, C., & Ong, C. (2004). *Towards the characterization of academic language in upper elementary science classrooms* (Center for the Study of Evaluation Report No. 621). Los Angeles: Graduate School of Education and Information Studies, University of California, Los Angeles.

Baker, E. A. (Ed.). (2010). *The new literacies: Multiple perspectives on research and practice*. New York: Guilford Press.

Barr, R., Kamil, M., Mosenthal, P., & Pearson, P. D. (Eds.). (1991). *Handbook of reading research* (Vol. 2). New York: Longman.

Barton, M., Heidema, C., & Jordan, D. (2002). Teaching reading in mathematics and science. *Educational Leadership, 50*(3), 24–28.

Baumann, J. F., Edwards, E. C., Boland, E., Olejnik, S., & Kame'enui, E. W. (2003). Vocabulary tricks: Effects of instruction in morphology and context on fifth-grade students' ability to derive and infer word meanings. *American Educational Research Journal, 40*, 447–494.

Baumann, J. F., Edwards, E. C., Font, G., Tereshinski, C., Kame'enui, E., & Olejnik, S. (2002). Teaching morphemic and contextual analysis to fifth-grade students. *Reading Research Quarterly, 372*, 150–176.

Baumann, J. F., & Graves, M. F. (2010). What is academic vocabulary? *Journal of Adolescent and Adult Literacy, 54*(1), 4–12.

Baumann, J. F., Kame'enui, E. J., & Ash, G. E. (2003). Research on vocabulary instruction: Voltaire redux. In J. Flood, D. Lapp, J. R. Squire, & J. M. Jensen (Eds.), *Handbook of research on teaching the English language arts* (2nd ed.). Mahwah, NJ: Erlbaum.

Baumann, J. F., Manyak, P. C., Peterson, H., Blachowicz, C. L. Z., Cieply, C., Bates, A., et al. (2011, December). *Windows on formative/design-based research on vocabulary instruction: Findings and methodological challenges.* Symposium conducted at the 61st Annual Conference of the Literacy Research Association, Jacksonville, FL.

Baumann, J. F., Ware, D., & Edwards, E. C. (2007). "Bumping into spicy, tasty words that catch your tongue": A formative experiment on vocabulary instruction. *The Reading Teacher, 62,* 108–122.

Beck, I. L., & McKeown, M. G. (1991). Conditions of vocabulary acquisition. In R. Barr, M. Kamil, P. Mosenthal, & P. D. Pearson (Eds.), *Handbook of reading research* (Vol. 2, pp. 789–814). New York: Longman.

Beck, I. L., & McKeown, M. G. (2007). Increasing young low-income children's oral vocabulary repertoires through rich and focused instruction. *Elementary School Journal, 107,* 251–271.

Beck, I. L., McKeown, M., & Kucan, L. (2002). *Bringing words to life: Robust vocabulary instruction.* New York: Guilford Press.

Beck, I. L., McKeown, M. G., & Kucan, L. (2013). *Bringing words to life: Robust vocabulary instruction* (2nd ed.). New York: Guilford Press.

Becker, W. C. (1977). Teaching reading and language to the disadvantaged—what we have learned from field research. *Harvard Educational Review, 47,* 518–543.

Bednarz, S., Clinton, C., Hartoonian, M., Hernandez, A., Marshall, P. L., & Nickell, P. (2003). *Discover our heritage.* Boston: Houghton Mifflin.

Berne, J., & Blachowicz, C. L. Z. (2009). What reading teachers say about vocabulary instruction: Voices from the classroom. *The Reading Teacher, 62*(4), 314–323

Bierwisch, M. (Ed.). (1983). *Pronominal reference: Child language and the theory of grammar.* Dordrecht, Netherlands: D. Reidel.

Besnoy, K. D., & Clarke, L. W. (Eds.). (2010). *High-tech teaching success!: A step-by-step guide to using innovative technology in your classroom.* Waco, TX: Prufrock Press.

Biemiller, A., & Boote, C. (2006). An effective method for building meaning vocabulary in primary grades. *Journal of Educational Psychology, 98,* 44–62.

Biemiller, A., & Slonim, N. (2001). Estimating root word vocabulary growth in normative and advantaged populations: Evidence for a common sequence of vocabulary acquisition. *Journal of Educational Psychology, 93,* 498–520.

Blachowicz, C. L. Z. (1987). Vocabulary instruction: What goes on in the classroom? *The Reading Teacher, 41,* 132–137.

Blachowicz, C. L. Z., Bates, A., & Cieply, C. (2011, May). Vocabulary framing. In C. L. Z. Blachowicz, J. F. Baumann, P. C. Manyak, A. Bates, & C. Cieply, *Boost vocabulary power in classrooms.* Symposium presented at the 56th Annual Convention of the International Reading Association, Orlando, FL.

Blachowicz, C. L. Z., & Baumann, J. F. (2013). Language standards for vocabulary. In L. M. Morrow, K. K. Wixson, & T. Shanahan (Eds.), *Teaching with the Common Core Standards for English language arts, grades 3–5* (pp. 131–153). New York: Guilford Press.

Blachowicz, C. L. Z., & Cobb, C. (2007). *Action tools: Vocabulary across the content areas.* Alexandria, VA: Association for Supervision and Curriculum Development.

Blachowicz, C. L. Z., & Fisher, P. (2000). Vocabulary instruction. In M. L. Kamil, P. B. Mosenthal, P. D. Pearson, & R. Barr (Eds.), *Handbook of reading research* (Vol. 3, pp. 503–523). Mahwah, NJ: Erlbaum.

Blachowicz, C. L. Z., & Fisher, P. (2010). *Teaching vocabulary in all classrooms* (4th ed.). Boston: Pearson/Allyn & Bacon.

Blachowicz, C. L. Z., & Obrochta, C. (2005). Vocabulary Visits: Developing primary content vocabulary. *The Reading Teacher, 59*(3), 262–269.

Blachowicz, C. L. Z., & Obrochta, C. (2007). "Tweaking practice": Modifying read-alouds to enhance content vocabulary learning in grade 1. In D. W. Rowe et al. (Eds.), *56th yearbook of the National Reading Conference* (pp. 111–121). Oak Creek, WI: National Reading Conference.

Blanton, L. (2011). Alexander Graham Bell: A great inventor. In *Scott Foresman reading street.* Glenview, IL: Pearson.

Bloom, B. (1956). *Taxonomy of educational objectives: The classification of educational goals*. New York: Longmans.

Boyne, J. (2006) *The boy in the striped pajamas*. New York: Random House.

Braun, P. (2010). Taking the time to read aloud. *Science Scope, 34*(2), 45–49.

Bravo, M. A., Hiebert, E. H., & Pearson, P. D. (2007). Tapping the linguistic resources of Spanish/English bilinguals: The role of cognates in science. In R. K. Wagner, A. Muse, & K. Tannenbaum (Eds.), *Vocabulary acquisition: Implications for reading comprehension* (pp. 140–156). New York: Guilford Press.

Britton, J. N. (1993). *Language and learning: The importance of speech in children's development* (2nd ed.). Portsmouth, NH: Heinemann.

Brown, J. (1996). *Invisible Stanley*. New York: HarperTrophy.

Burleigh, R. (1997). *Hoops*. Orlando, FL: Harcourt Brace.

Bus, A. G., van IJzendoorn, M. H., & Pellegrini, A. D. (1995). Join book reading makes for success in learning to read: A meta-analysis on intergenerational transmission of *literacy. Review of Educational Research, 65*, 1–21.

Butler, F. A., Bailey, A. L., Stevens, R., & Huang, B. (2004). *Academic English in fifth-grade mathematics, science, and social studies textbooks* (Center for the Study of Evaluation Report No. 642). Los Angeles: Graduate School of Education and Information Studies, University of California, Los Angeles.

Carrier, K. A., & Tatum, A. W. (2006). Creating sentence walls to help English-language learners develop content literacy. *Reading Teacher, 60*, 285–288.

Cassie, B., & Pallotta, J. (1995). *The butterfly alphabet book*. Watertown, MA: Charlesbridge.

Celano, D., & Neuman, S. B. (2010). Roadblocks on the information highway. *Educational Leadership, 68*, 50–53.

Chamot, A. U., & O'Malley, M. J. (1994). *CALLA handbook: Implementing the cognitive academic language learning approach*. Reading, MA: Addison-Wesley.

Christ, T. (2007). *Oral language exposure and incidental vocabulary acquisition: An exploration across kindergarten classrooms*. Unpublished doctoral dissertation, State University of New York at Buffalo. (UMI No. 3262025)

Cleary, B. P. (2006). *A lime, a mime, a pool of slime: More about nouns*. Minneapolis, MN: Millbrook.

Cobb, C. (2003). *Academic vocabulary project*. Unpublished manuscript.

Coiro, J. (2005). Making sense of online text. *Educational Leadership, 63*(2), 30–35.

Coiro, J., Knobel, M., Lankshear, C., & Leu, D. J., (Eds.). (2008). *Handbook of research on new literacies*. New York: Erlbaum.

Coleman, R., & Goldenberg, C. (2010). What does research say about effective practice for English learners? *Kappa Delta Pi Record, 46*(2), 60–65.

Collins, M. F. (2010). ELL preschoolers' English vocabulary acquisition from storybook reading. *Early Childhood Research Quarterly, 25*, 84–97.

Coxhead, A. (2000). A new academic word list. *TESOL Quarterly, 34*(2), 213–238.

Crane, C. (2006). *D is for dancing dragon: A China alphabet*. Chelsea, MI: Sleeping Bear Press.

Cummins, J. (2000). *Language, power and pedagogy: Bilingual children in the crossfire*. Buffalo, NY: Multilingual Matters.

Cunningham, A. E. (2005). Vocabulary growth through independent reading and reading aloud to children. In E. H. Hiebert & M. L. Kamil (Eds.), *Teaching and learning vocabulary: Bringing research to practice* (pp. 45–68). Mahwah, NJ: Erlbaum.

Cunningham, A. E., & Stanovich, K. E. (1998). What reading does for the mind. *American Educator, 22*, 8–15.

Dale, E., & O'Rourke, J.P. (1976). *The living word vocabulary*. Chicago: Field Enterprises.

Dalton, B., & Grisham, D. L. (2011). eVoc strategies: 10 ways to use technology to build vocabulary. *The Reading Teacher, 64*, 306–317.

Damico, J. S., & Baildon, M. (2011). Content literacy for the 21st century: Excavation, elevation, and relational cosmopolitanism in the classroom. *Journal of Adolescent and Adult Literacy, 55*, 232–243.

Darling-Hammond, L., Wei, R. C., Andree, A., Richardson, N., & Orphanos, S. (2009). *Professional* learning in the learning professions: A status report on teacher development in the United States and abroad. Palo Alto, CA: School Redesign Network.

D'Anna, C. A., Zechmeister, E. B., & Hall, J. W. (1991). Toward a meaningful definition of vocabulary size. *Journal of Reading Behavior, 23,* 109–122.

D'Aulaire, I. (1962). *D'Aulaires' book of Greek myths.* Garden City, NY: Doubleday.

Dickinson, D. K., & Smith, M. W. (1994). Long-term effects of preschool teachers' book readings on low-income children's vocabulary and story comprehension. *Reading Research Quarterly, 29,* 104–122.

Dimino, J., & Taylor, M. J. (2009). *Learning how to improve vocabulary instruction through teacher study groups.* Baltimore, MD: Brookes.

Dodge, A. M., Husain, N., & Duke, N. K. (2011). Connected kids?: K–2 children's use and understanding of the Internet. *Language Arts, 89*(2), 86–98.

Donnelly, W. B., & Roe, C. J. (2010). Using sentence frames to develop academic vocabulary for English learners. *The Reading Teacher, 64,* 131–136.

Draper, S. M. (2002). *Double Dutch.* New York: Simon & Schuster.

Duke, N. K. (2004). The case for informational text. *Educational Leadership, 61*(6), 40–44.

Eagleton, M. B., & Guinee, K. (2002). Strategies for supporting student Internet inquiry. *New England Reading Association Journal, 38*(2), 39–47.

Echeveria, J., Vogt, M. E., & Short, K. (2012). *Making content comprehensible for English learners: The SIOP model.* Boston: Pearson.

Edley, J., & the Creators of Bananagrams. (2009). *Bananagrams!: The official book.* New York: Workman.

Eller, G., Pappas, C. C., & Brown, E. (1988). The lexical development of kindergartners: Learning from written context. *Journal of Reading Behavior, 20,* 5–24.

Elley, W. B. (1989). Vocabulary acquisition from listening to stories. *Reading Research Quarterly, 24,* 174–187.

Evans, K. (2002). Fifth-grade students' perceptions of how they experience literature discussion groups. *Reading Research Quarterly, 37*(1), 46–69.

Fang, Z., & Schleppegrell, M. J. (2010). Disciplinary literacies across content areas: Supporting secondary reading through functional language analysis. *Journal of Adolescent and Adult Literacy, 53,* 587–597.

Fang, Z., Schleppegrell, M. J., & Cox, B. E. (2006). Understanding the language demands of schooling: Nouns in academic registers. *Journal of Literacy Research, 38*(3), 247–273.

Farris, C. K. (2003). *My brother Martin: A sister remembers growing up with the Rev. Dr. Martin Luther King, Jr.* New York: Simon & Schuster.

Farstrup, A. E., & Samuels, S. J. (Eds.). (2008). *What research has to say about vocabulary instruction.* Newark, DE: International Reading Association.

Fisher, D., & Frey, N. (2008). *Word wise and content rich: Five essential steps to teaching academic vocabulary.* Portsmouth, NH: Heinemann.

Fisher, D., & Frey, N. (2010). Unpacking the language purpose: Vocabulary, structure and function. *TESOL Journal, 1*(3), 315–337.

Fisher, P. J., Blachowicz, C. L. Z., & Smith, J. C. (1991). Vocabulary learning in literature discussion groups. In J. Zutell & S. McCormick (Eds.), *Learner factors/teacher factors: Issues in literacy research and instruction.* Fortieth yearbook of the National Reading Conference (pp. 201–209). Chicago: National Reading Conference.

Fogelberg, E., Skalinder, C., Satz, P., Hiller, B., Bernstein, L., & Vitantonio, S. (2008). *Integrating literacy and math: Strategies for K–6 teachers.* New York: Guilford Press.

Fountas, I., & Pinnell, G. S. (1996). *Guided reading: Good first teaching for all children.* Portsmouth, NH: Heinemann.

Frazier, D. (2000). *Miss Alaineus: A vocabulary disaster.* San Diego, CA: Harcourt Brace.

Frey, N., & Fisher, D. (2009). *Learning words inside and out.* Portsmouth, NH: Heinemann.

Fukkink, R. G., & de Glopper, K. (1998). Effects of instruction in deriving word meaning from context: A meta-analysis. *Review of Educational Research, 68,* 450–469.

Gambrell, L. B. Malloy, J. A., & Mazzoni, S. A. (2011). Evidence-based best practice in comprehensive literacy instruction. In L. M. Morrow & L. B. Gambrell (Eds.), *Best practices in literacy instruction* (4th ed., pp. 11–36). New York: Guilford Press.

Giff, P. R. (2002). *Pictures of Hollis Woods*. New York: Random House.

Gill, S. R. (2007). Learning about word parts with Kidspiration. *The Reading Teacher, 61,* 79–84.

Glover, D. (1997). *Ramps and wedges*. Crystal Lake, IL: Rigby Interactive Library.

Graves, M. F. (1986). Vocabulary learning and instruction. In E. Z. Rothkopf (Ed.), *Review of research in education* (Vol. 13, pp. 49–89). Washington, DC: American Educational Research Association.

Graves, M. F. (2006). *The vocabulary book: Learning and instruction*. New York: Teachers College Press.

Graves, M. F. (Ed.). (2009). *Essential readings on vocabulary instruction*. Newark, DE: International Reading Association.

Graves, M. F., & Watts-Taffe, S. M. (2002). The place of word consciousness in a research-based vocabulary program. In A. E. Farstrup & S. J. Samuels (Eds.), *What research has to say about reading instruction* (3rd ed., pp. 140–165). Newark, DE: International Reading Association.

Haas, M. E. (1988). *An analysis of the social science and history concepts in elementary social studies textbooks grades 1–4*. Paper presented at the annual meeting of the National Council for the Social Studies. (ERIC Document Reproduction Service No. ED 305310)

Haggard, M. R. (1982). The vocabulary self-collection strategy: An active approach to word learning. *Journal of Reading, 26,* 203–207.

Halliday, M., & Hasan, R. (1989). *Language, context, and text: Aspects of language in a social-semiotic perspective*. Oxford, UK: Oxford University Press.

Harcourt Brace. (1995). *Treasury of literature, grade 4* (Vol. 2). Orlando, FL: Author.

Haring, K. (1998). *Big*. New York: Hyperion.

Harmon, J. M., Hedrick, W. B., & Fox, E. A. (2000) A content analysis of vocabulary instruction in social studies textbooks for grades 4–8. *Elementary School Journal, 100,* 253–271.

Harmon, J. M., Hedrick, W. B., Wood, K. D., & Gress, M. (2005). Vocabulary self-selection: A study of middle-school students' word selections from expository texts. *Reading Psychology, 26,* 313–333.

Harris, A. J., & Jacobson, M. D. (1982). *Basic reading vocabularies*. New York: Macmillan.

Hart, B., & Risley, T. R. (1995). *Meaningful differences in the everyday experience of young American children*. Baltimore, MD: Brookes.

Heller, R. (1987) *A cache of jewels*. New York: Grosset & Dunlap.

Heller, R. (1988). *Kites sail high*. New York: Grosset & Dunlap.

Henkes, K. (1993). *Owen*. New York: Greenwillow Books.

Henry, L. A. (2006). SEARCHing for an answer: The critical role of new literacies while reading the Internet. *The Reading Teacher, 59,* 614–627.

Hiebert, E. H., & Cervetti, G. N. (2012). What differences in narrative and informational texts mean for the learning and instruction of vocabulary. In E. J. Kame'enui & J. F. Baumann (Eds.), *Vocabulary instruction: Research to practice* (2nd ed., pp. 322–334). New York: Guilford Press.

Hiebert, E. H., & Kamil, M. L. (Eds.). (2005). *Teaching and learning vocabulary: Bringing research to practice*. Mahwah, NJ: Erlbaum.

Hiebert, E. H., & Lubliner, S. (2008). The nature, learning, and instruction of general academic vocabulary. In A. E. Farstrup & S. J. Samuels (Eds.), *What research has to say about vocabulary instruction* (pp. 106–129). Newark, DE: International Reading Association.

Hyde, A. (2006). *Comprehending math: Adapting reading strategies to teach mathematics, K–6*. Portsmouth, NH: Heinemann.

Hyland, K., & Tse, P. (2007). Is there an "academic vocabulary"? *TESOL Quarterly, 41*(2), 235–253.

Ikpeze, C. H., & Boyd, F. B. (2007). Web-based inquiry learning: Facilitating thoughtful literacy with WebQuests. *The Reading Teacher, 60,* 644–654.

Institute for Educational Leadership. (2000). *Leadership for student learning: Reinventing the principalship* (School Leadership for the 21st Century Initiative: A Report of the Task Force on the Principalship). Washington, DC: Author.

International Society for Technology in Education. (2007). *National educational technology standards for students*. Washington, DC: Author.

Jolongo, M. R. (2008). *Learning to listen, listening to learn: Building essential skills in young children*. Washington, DC: National Association for the Education of Young Children.

Kame'enui, E. J., & Baumann, J. F. (Eds.). (2012). *Vocabulary instruction: Research to practice* (2nd ed.). New York: Guilford Press.

Kieffer, M., & Lesaux, N. (2007). Breaking down words to build meaning: Morphology, vocabulary, and reading comprehension in the urban classroom. *The Reading Teacher, 61*, 134–144.

Kim, J. S., & White, T. G. (2008). Scaffolding voluntary summer reading for children in grades 3 to 5: An experimental study. *Scientific Studies of Reading, 12*, 1–23.

Kimmel, E. C. (1999). *Balto and the great race*. New York: Random House.

Lesaux, N. K., Kieffer, M. J., Faller, S. E., & Kelley, J. G. (2010). The effectiveness and ease of implementation of an academic English vocabulary intervention for linguistically diverse students in urban middle schools. *Reading Research Quarterly, 45*, 196–228.

Leu, D. J., Coiro, J., Castek, J., Hartman, D. K., Henry, L. A., & Reinking, D. (2008). Research on instruction and assessment in the new literacies of online reading comprehension. In C. C. Block & S. Parris (Eds.), *Comprehension instruction: Research-based best practices* (2nd ed., pp. 321–346). New York: Guilford Press.

Leu, D. J., Leu, D. D., & Coiro, J. (2004), *Teaching with the Internet K–12: New literacies for new times* (4th ed.). Norwood, MA: Christopher Gordon.

Leu, D. J., McVerry, G., O'Byrne, W. I., Zawalinski, L., Castek, J., & Hartman, D. K. (2009). The new literacies of online reading comprehension and the irony of No Child Left Behind: Students who require our assistance the most actually receive it the least. In L. M. Morrow, R. Rueda, & D. Lapp (Eds.), *Handbook of research on literacy and diversity: Issues of diversity, policy, and equity* (pp. 173–194). New York: Guilford Press.

Lewis, C. S. (1950). *The lion, the witch and the wardrobe*. New York: Macmillan.

Lubinsky, J. (2010). It all adds up!: Using technology in the math classroom. In K. D. Besnoy & L. W. Clarke (Eds.), *High-tech teaching success!: A step-by-step guide to using innovating technology in your classroom* (pp. 20–69). Waco, TX: Prufrock Press.

Lubliner, S., & Scott, J. A., (2008). *Nourishing vocabulary: Balancing words and learning*. Thousand Oaks, CA: Corwin Press.

Luke, G., & Quinn, S. (2003). *Americanisms: The illustrated book of words made in the USA*. Seattle, WA: Sasquatch Books.

Manyak, P. (2007). Character trait vocabulary: A schoolwide approach. *The Reading Teacher, 60*, 574–577.

Marcus, J. (2008). What's in your iPod?: Mixing music and meaning. *Middle Ground, 12*(1), 19–21.

Maria, K., & MacGinitie, W. (1987). Learning from texts that refute the reader's prior knowledge. *Reading Research and Instruction, 26*, 222–238.

Marsalis, W. (2005). *Jazz A-B-Z*. Cambridge, MA: Candlewick.

Marshall, N. (1989). Overcoming problems with incorrect prior knowledge: An instructional study. In S. McCormick & J. Zutell (Eds.), *Cognitive and social perspectives for literacy research and instruction*. Thirty-eighth Yearbook of the National Reading Conference. Chicago: National Reading Conference.

Mattel Corporation. (1999). *Apples to apples*. El Segundo, CA: Author.

Marzano, R. J. (2004). *Building background knowledge for academic achievement*. Alexandria, VA: Association for Supervision and Curriculum Development.

Marzano, R. J., & Pickering, D. (2005). *Building academic vocabulary*. Alexandria, VA: Association for Supervision and Curriculum Development.

McKeown, M. G., & Beck, I. L. (1988). Learning vocabulary: Different ways for different goals. *Remedial and Special Education, 9*, 42–45.

McKeown, M. G., & Beck, I. L. (1989). *The assessment and characterization of young learners' knowledge of a topic in history*. Paper presented at the National Reading Conference, San Antonio, TX.

McKeown, M. G., & Beck, I. L. (2004). Direct and rich vocabulary instruction. In J. F. Baumann and E. J. Kame'enui (Eds.), *Vocabulary instruction* (pp. 13–27). New York: Guilford Press,

McKeown, M. G., Beck, I. L., Omanson, R. C., & Pople, M. T. (1985). Some effects of the nature and frequency of vocabulary instruction on the knowledge and use of words. *Reading Research Quarterly, 20*, 522–535.

Mezynski, K. (1983). Issues concerning the acquisition of knowledge: Effects of vocabulary training on reading comprehension. *Review of Educational Research, 53*, 253–279.

Nagy, W. E. (1988). *Teaching vocabulary to improve comprehension.* Newark, DE: International Reading Association.

Nagy, W. E. (2005). Why vocabulary instruction needs to be long-term and comprehensive. In E. H. Hiebert & M. L. Kamil (Eds.), *Teaching and learning vocabulary: Bringing research to practice* (pp. 27–44). Mahwah, NJ: Erlbaum.

Nagy, W. E., & Anderson, R. C. (1984). How many words are there in printed school English? *Reading Research Quarterly, 19*, 303–330.

Nagy, W. E., Anderson, R. C., & Herman, P. A. (1987). Learning word meanings from context during normal reading. *American Educational Research Journal, 24*, 237–270.

Nagy, W. E., & Herman, P. A. (1987). Breadth and depth of vocabulary knowledge: Implications for acquisition and instruction. In M. G. McKeown & M. E. Curtis (Eds.), *The nature of vocabulary acquisition* (pp. 19–35). Hillsdale, NJ: Erlbaum.

Nagy, W. E., Herman, P. A., & Anderson, R. C. (1985). Learning words from context. *Reading Research Quarterly, 20*, 233–253.

Nagy, W. E., & Scott, J. A. (2000). Vocabulary processes. In M. L. Kamil, P. B. Mosenthal, P. D. Pearson, & R. Barr (Eds.), *Handbook of reading research* pp. (Vol. 3, pp. 269–284). Mahwah, NJ: Erlbaum.

Nagy, W., & Townsend, D. (2012). Words as tools: Learning academic vocabulary as language acquisition. *Reading Research Quarterly. 47*(1), 91–109.

National Governors Association (NGO) & Council of Chief State School Officers (CCSSO). (2010). *Common Core State Standards for English language arts and literacy in history/social studies, science, and technical subjects.* Washington, DC: Authors.

Neugebauer, S. R., & Currie-Rubin, R. (2009). Read-alouds in Calca, Peru: A bilingual indigenous context. *The Reading Teacher, 62*(5), 396–405.

Newman, F. R. (1983). *ZOUNDS! The kids' guide to sound making.* New York: Random House.

Nussbaum, J. (1979). Children's conceptions of the earth as a cosmic body: A cross-age study. *Science Education, 63*, 83–93.

Nussbaum, J., & Novick, S. (1982). Alternative frameworks, conceptual conflict and accommodation: Toward a principled teaching strategy. *Instructional Science, 11*(3), 183–200.

Ogle, D. (1986). K-W-L: A teaching model that develops active reading of expository text. *Reading Teacher, 39*, 564–570.

Ogle, D. (2011). *Partnering for content literacy: PRC2 in action.* Boston: Pearson.

Ogle, D., & Correa-Kovtun, A. (2010). Supporting English language learners and struggling readers with the Partner Reading and Content, Too routine. *The Reading Teacher, 63*(7), 532–542.

Ogle, D., Klemp, R., & McBride, W. (2007). *Building literacy in social studies.* Alexandria, VA: Association for Supervision and Curriculum Development.

Ohio Department of Education. (2011). Ohio revised science standards and model curriculum: Grades preK through eight. Retrieved December 10, 2012, from *www.ode.state.oh.us.*

Passig, D. (2003). A taxonomy of future higher thinking skills. *Informatics in Education, 2*, 79–92. Retrieved October 4, 2011, from *http://dl.acm.org/citation.cfm?id=937521.*

Programme for International Student Assessment (PISA). (2012). PISA 2009 technical report. Paris: Organisation for Economic Co-operation and Development (OECD). Retrieved from *www.oecd.org/dataoecd/60/31/50036771.pdf.*

Prensky, M. (2001). Digital natives, digital immigrants. *On the Horizon, 9*, 1–6.

Putnam, S. M., & Kingsley, T. (2009). The atoms family: Using podcasts to enhance the development of science vocabulary. *The Reading Teacher, 63*, 100–108.

Rasinski, T. V., Padak, N., Newton, J., & Newton, E. (2011). The Latin–Greek connection: Building vocabulary through morphological study. *The Reading Teacher, 65*, 133–141.

Ray, K. W. (1999). *Wondrous words: Writers and writing in the elementary classroom*. Urbana, IL: National Council of Teachers of English.

Rideout, V. J., Foehr, U., G., & Roberts, D., F. (2010). *Generation M²: Media in the lives of 8–18-year-olds*. Menlo Park, CA: Kaiser Family Foundation. Retrieved from *www.kff.org/entmedia/upload/8010.pdf*.

Roman, L., & Roman, M. (2010). *Encyclopedia of Greek and Roman mythology*. New York: Facts on File.

Roop, P., & Roop, C. (1985). *Keep the lights burning, Abbie*. Minneapolis, MN: Carolrhoda Books.

Ross, D., Fisher, D., & Frey, N. (2009). The art of argumentation. *Science and Children, 47*(3), 28–31.

Ruddell, R. B. (1999). *Teaching children to read and write: Becoming an influential teacher* (2nd ed.). Boston: Allyn & Bacon.

Sarafini, F. (2001). *The reading workshop: Creating space for readers*. Portsmouth, NH: Heinemann.

Schatz, D. (2009). *Stereobook: Dinosaurs*. San Francisco: Chronicle Books.

Schleppegrell, M. J. (2004). *The language of schooling: A functional linguistic perspective*. Mahwah, NJ: Erlbaum.

Schwartz, D. M. (2001) *Q is for quark: A science alphabet*. Berkeley, CA: Tricycle Press.

Scieszka, J. (2005) *Baloney (Henry P.)*. New York: Viking.

Scott, J. A., Flinspach, S. L., & Vevea, J. L. (2011). *Identifying and teaching vocabulary in fourth- and fifth-grade math and science*. Paper presented at the 61st Annual Conference of the Literacy Research Association, Jacksonville, FL.

Scott, J. A., Jamieson-Noel, D., & Asselin, M. (2003). Vocabulary instruction throughout the day in twenty-three Canadian upper-elementary classrooms. *Elementary School Journal, 103*, 269–286.

Scott, J. A., Miller, T. F., & Flinspach, S. L. (2012). Developing word consciousness: Lessons from highly diverse fourth-grade classrooms. In E. J. Kame'enui & J. F. Baumann (Eds.). *Vocabulary instruction: Research to practice* (2nd ed., pp. 169–188). New York: Guilford Press.Scott, J. A., & Nagy, W. E. (1997). Understanding the definitions of unfamiliar verbs. *Reading Research Quarterly, 32*, 184–200.

Scott, J. A., Nagy, W. E., & Flinspach, S. L. (2008). More than merely words: Redefining vocabulary learning in a culturally and linguistically diverse society. In A. E. Farstrup & S. J. Samuels (Eds.), *What research has to say about vocabulary instruction* (pp. 182–210). Newark, DE: International Reading Association.

Scott, J. A., Skobel, B. J., & Wells, J. (2008). *The word-conscious classroom: Building the vocabulary readers and writers need*. New York: Scholastic.

Semetsky, I. (2006, June). Semanalysis in the age of abjection. *Applied Semiotics/Sémiotique Appliqué*, No. 17, 24–38.

Sendak, M. (1963). *Where the wild things are*. New York: Harper & Row.

Seuss, Dr. [T. S. Geisel]. (1960). *Green eggs and ham*. New York: Random House.

Silver Burdett & Ginn. (1991). *Science horizons, grade 2*. New York: Authors.

Stahl, S. A., & Fairbanks, M. M. (1986). The effects of vocabulary instruction: A model-based meta-analysis. *Review of Educational Research, 56*, 72–110.

Stahl, S. A., & Nagy, W. E. (2006). *Teaching word meanings*. Mahwah, NJ: Erlbaum.

Strickland, D., & Riley-Ayers, S. (2006). *Early literacy: Policy and practice in the preschool years*. New Brunswick, NJ: National Institute for Early Education Research.

Swanborn, M. S. L., & de Glopper, K. (1999). Incidental word learning while reading: A meta-analysis. *Review of Educational Research, 69*, 261–285.

Tomeson, M., & Aarnoutse, C. (1998). Effects of an instructional programme for deriving word meanings. *Educational Studies, 24*, 107–128.

Tomlinson, C. (2001). *How to differentiate instruction in mixed ability classrooms* (2nd ed.). Alexandria, VA: Association for Supervision and Curriculum Development.

U.S. Department of Education. (2001). Elementary and secondary education: Part D. Enhancing education through technology. Retrieved from *www2.ed.gov/policy/elsec/leg/esea02/pg34.html.*

van Kleeck, A., Stahl, S., & Bauer, E. (Eds.). (2003). *On reading books to children: Parents and teachers,* Mahwah, NJ: Erlbaum.

Vandewater, E., Rideout, V., Wartella, E., Huang, X., Lee, J., & Shim, M. (2007). Digital childhood: Electronic media and technology use among infants, toddlers, and preschoolers. *Pediatrics, 119,* e1006–e1015.

Verstraete, L. (2011) *S is for scientists.* Chelsea, MI: Sleeping Bear Press.

Vosniadou, S., & Ortony, A. (1983). The emergence of the literal–metaphorical–anomalous distinction in young children. *Child Development, 54,* 154–161.

Watkins. P. A., & Leto, G. K. (1994). *Life science.* Austin, TX: Holt Rhinehart & Winston.

Watts, S. M. (1991). *Vocabulary instruction across homogeneous ability groups in grades five and six.* Unpublished doctoral dissertation, State University of New York at Buffalo. (UMI No. 9210660)

Watts, S. M., & Truscott, D. M. (1996). Using contextual analysis to help students become independent word learners. *New England Reading Association Journal, 32*(3), 13–20.

Watts-Taffe, S. (2008, May). *Using rich conversation and structured academic routines for vocabulary development in preschool and the primary grades.* Paper presented at the annual meeting of the International Reading Association, Atlanta, GA.

Watts Taffe, S., & Bauer, L. B. (2013). Digital literacy. In B. M. Taylor & N. Duke (Eds.), *Handbook of effective literacy instruction: Research-based practice K–8* (pp. 162–188). New York: Guilford Press.

Watts Taffe, S., Blachowicz, C. L. Z., & Fisher, P. J. (2009). Vocabulary instruction for diverse students. In L. M. Morrow, R. Rueda, & D. Lapp (Eds.), *Handbook of research on literacy and diversity* (pp. 320–336). New York: Guilford Press.

White, E. B. (1952). *Charlotte's web.* New York: Harper & Row.

White, T. G., Graves, M. F., & Slater, W. H. (1990). Growth of reading vocabulary in diverse elementary schools: Decoding and word meaning. *Journal of Educational Psychology, 82,* 281–290.

Whittlesea, B. W. (1987). Preservation of specific experiences in the representation of general knowledge. *Journal of Experimental Psychology: Learning, Memory, and Cognition, 13*(1), 3–17.

Wieland, K.M. (2008, December). *A study of excellent readers thinking aloud during CVA.* In S. Watts-Taffe (Chair), Acquiring a sense of a word's meaning from verbal context: Processes, outcomes, and curricular directions. Symposium presented at the annual meeting of National Reading Conference, Orlando, FL.

Willoughby, S., Bereiter, C., Hilton, P., & Rubinstein, J. H.(2007). *SRA Real Math.* Chicago: Science Research Associates.

Wray, D. (2001). *Developing factual writing: An approach through scaffolding.* Paper presented at the European Reading Conference, Dublin, Ireland.

Wright, T. (2012). What classroom observations reveal about classroom vocabulary instruction. *Reading Research Quarterly. 47*(4), 353–355.

Zhang, S., & Duke, N. K. (2011). The impact of instruction in the WWWDOT framework on students' disposition and ability to evaluate web sites as sources of information. *Elementary School Journal, 112*(1), 132–154.

Zwiers, J. (2008). *Building academic language: Essential practices in content classrooms.* San Francisco: Jossey-Bass.

Index

Page numbers followed by *f* indicate figure; *t* indicate table